California Wine Winners

1993

Results of the 1992 Wine Judgings

Edited by
TRUDY AHLSTROM
and
J.T. DEVINE

Printed in the United States of America
by Delta Lithograph Company

ISBN 0-9614025-9-8
ISSN 0883-4423

To order additional copies of this book or copies of any of the previous nine editions, please send:
$8.45 for the 1992 or 1991 results;
$7.45 for the results of any years between 1983 and 1990.

VARIETAL FAIR
4022 Harrison Grade Road
Sebastopol, CA 95472
707 • 874 • 3105

TABLE OF CONTENTS

THE COMPETITIONS

Los Angeles County Fair
Orange County Fair
Riverside Farmers Fair
San Francisco Fair
Dallas Morning News
California State Fair
National Orange Show
West Coast Competition
San Diego Competition

THE VARIETALS

Cabernet Sauvignon
Chardonnay
Chenin Blanc
Gewurztraminer
Johannisberg Riesling
Merlot
Petite Sirah
Pinot Noir
Red Meritage
Sauvignon (Fume) Blanc
Sparkling Wine
White Meritage
White Zinfandel
Zinfandel

INTRODUCTION

The purpose of this book is to provide one pocket-size guide to all the California wines that won medals in this year's competitions. The nine competitions covered and the twelve varietals included are listed on the facing page.

ORGANIZATION

The book is divided into two parts. The first part lists the award winners under specific varietals. Each varietal section is subdivided into groups of nine award winners, eight award winners, seven award winners, etc. The wines are listed alphabetically within those subdivisions, and identified by vintage, appellation and price. Across from each wine a **G** (gold), **S** (silver), or **B** (bronze) shows what award was won in each of the competitions.

Johannisberg Riesling, Gewurztraminer and Sparkling Wines are further broken down into residual sugar classes, and higher residual sugar wines have their "R.S.___" noted.

The second part of the book is an alphabetical listing of all the winning wineries including their addresses. Under each name, the winning wines are listed with the number of awards indicated in parenthesis so they can be easily found in the front section. Single-medal winners are listed only in the back, with the award and competition identified.

SAMPLE FRONT SECTION

Sparkling Wine 0 - 1.5 Residual Sugar	L.A.	Orange	Farmers	San Fran	Dallas	State Fair	Nat'l O.S.	W. Coast	San Diego
8 AWARDS CHATEAU DE BAUN WINERY '88, Sonoma Co., Rhapsody, Brut $11.00	S	G	B	S		S	S	B	G
7 AWARDS BALLATORE CHAMPAGNE CELLARS 'NV, California, Gran Spumante $5.50	S	S	B	G		B	S		B

VARIETAL
NUMBER OF AWARDS
WINERY
PRICE
APPELLATION
YEAR
SILVER MEDAL
BRONZE MEDAL
GOLD MEDAL

WINE JUDGINGS
L.A. — Los Angeles County Fair
Orange — Orange County Fair
Farmers — Riverside Farmers Fair
San Fran — San Francisco Fair
Dallas — Dallas Morning News
State Fair — California State Fair
Nat'l O.S. — National Orange Show
W. Coast — West Coast Competition
San Diego — San Diego Competition

SAMPLE BACK SECTION

WINERY (listed alphabetically)

ADDRESS (All cities in California)

VARIETAL (followed by year, appellation, and price)

NUMBER OF AWARDS (cross reference to front section)

SINGLE AWARD WINES SHOWN WITH MEDAL AND COMPETITION

A

ABBEY D'OR

4620 Hog Canyon Rd. San Miguel 93451

Cabernet Scuvignon,'87, Paso Robles (2)

ACACIA

2750 Las Amigas Road Napa 94558

Chardonnay,'90, Napa Vly., Carneros (2)
Pinot Noir,'90, Napa Vly., Carneros (S-Orange)

ADELAIDA CELLARS

2170 Adelaida Star Rd. Paso Robles 93446

Cabernet Sauvignon,'88, Paso Robles $14.50 (2)
Chardonnay,'90, Paso Robles (2)
Zinfandel,'89, Paso Robles $12.00 (3)

COMPETITIONS

The competitions start in February and last until August. Some wines can't be entered in all the judgings simply because the January entries are sold out by the end of summer. Some wineries, for whatever reason, choose not to enter their wines in competition. The entry requirements for the competitions vary, as do the categories within which they choose to judge. That information is summarized on the following page.

POINT COUNTS & REGION COMPARISONS

We have added a page at the beginning of each section that ranks the top dozen or so winners by weighting the value of each award. Gold = 5 points, Silver = 3 points, and Bronze = 1. The values are arbitrary; it is just another way of looking at the awards. Also included is a graph that shows which regions of the state took how many points of those weighted medals. The regions refer to those areas where the grapes were grown, not necessarily where the wineries are located:

North Coast .... Lake, Mendocino, Marin and Solano Counties.
Sonoma .... Sonoma County (11 Appellations).
Napa .... Napa County (5 Appellations).
Bay Area .... Santa Clara, Santa Cruz, Alameda Counties.
No. Central Coast .... Monterey and San Benito Counties.
So. Central Coast ..... San Luis Obispo and Santa Barbara Counties.
South Coast .... L.A., Orange, Riverside, San Diego and Ventura Counties.
Sierra Foothills .... Amador, Calaveras, El Dorado, Nevada, Placer and Tuolomne Counties.
Other .... All other California Counties
California .... Non-specified blends from above appellations.

COMPETITION JUDGING DATES	ENTRIES # Wineries # in Calif. #Wines	MEDALS Total # in this book	ENTRY REQUIREMENTS AND RESTRICTIONS
LOS ANGELES COUNTY FAIR July 22 - 25	396 ?-CA 1767	554 373	Any wine from any of the American continents.
ORANGE COUNTY FAIR May 30 - 31	503 2528	1072 850	All California wines available in Orange County. 1 entry per class Judged within price categories.
FARMERS FAIR RIVERSIDE May 2 - 3	273 1302	508 435	Any bonded winery in California. Limit of 15 entries.
SAN FRANCISCO FAIR June 11 - 13	420 ?-CA 1917	590 393	Any U.S. wine.. Not all entries voluntary.
DALLAS MORNING NEWS Feb. 14 - 16	322 253-CA 1384	476 281	Any U.S. wine. Limit of 3 entries per category.
CALIFORNIA STATE FAIR July 10 - 12	411 1798	518 414	All California wine. Limit of 2 entries per class. Wines judged in 10 geo graphical groupings.
NATIONAL ORANGE SHOW Feb. 27 - 28	373 283-CA 1750	605 359	Any wine from the "New World" countries. No limit on number of entries.
WEST COAST COMPETITION May 6 - 8	273 239-CA 1196	471 379	Any wine from the Western U.S.
SAN DIEGO COMPETITION Apr. 25 - 26	425 ?-CA 1823	675 440	Any U.S.vinifera wine. No limit on number of entries.

K-J
VINEYARDS AND WINERY
PROPRIETOR'S GRAND RESERVE
KENDALL-JACKSON
1987
Cabernet Sauvignon
CALIFORNIA
ALCOHOL 12.5% BY VOLUME

SIGNORELLO

Cabernet Sauvignon

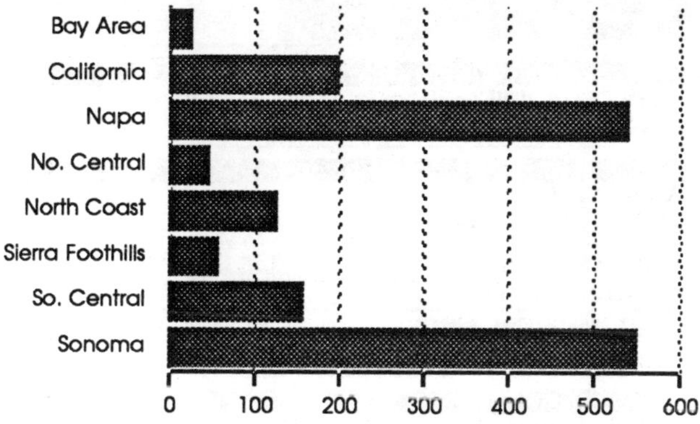

Regional Comparison of Total Points

(Gold=5 Silver=3 Bronze=1)

Highest individual wine totals

23	**KENDALL-JACKSON WINERY** '87, Calif., Prop. Grand Reserve $22.50
22	**SIGNORELLO VINEYARDS** '89, Napa Vly., Founder's Reserve $25.00
21	**CHATEAU ST. JEAN** '88, Sonoma Co. $18.00
21	**GOLDEN CREEK VINEYARD** '89, Sonoma Co. $12.00
20	**MERIDIAN VINEYARDS** '89, Paso Robles $12.00
19	**KENDALL-JACKSON WINERY** '89, California, Vintner's Reserve $13.00
19	**GEYSER PEAK WINERY** '89, Alexander Vly. $9.00
18	**VILLA MT. EDEN WINERY** '88, California, Cellar Select $9.00
18	**BENZIGER OF GLEN ELLEN** '89, Sonoma Co. $12.00
17	**NAVARRO VINEYARDS** '87, Mendocino $16.00
17	**CASTORO CELLARS** '89, Paso Robles $10.00
17	**CLOS DU BOIS** '88, Alexander Vly., Briarcrest $21.00

Cabernet Sauvignon

Wine	L.A.	Orange	Farmers	San Fran	Dallas	State Fair	Nat'l O.S.	W. Coast	San Diego
9 AWARDS									
GOLDEN CREEK VINEYARD '89, Sonoma Co. $12.00	B	G	B	B	S	B	G	S	B
7 AWARDS									
CHATEAU ST. JEAN '88, Sonoma Co. $18.00	G			S	G	B	G	B	B
GEYSER PEAK WINERY '89, Alexander Vly. $9.00		G		G	G	B	B	B	B
KENDALL-JACKSON WINERY '87, Calif., Prop. Grand Reserve $22.50	G	G		B	B	B	G	G	
6 AWARDS									
BENZIGER OF GLEN ELLEN '89, Sonoma Co. $12.00		S	G	S	B		B		G
BYRON VINEYARD '89, Santa Barbara Co. $16.00	S			S	B	B	S	G	
CONN CREEK WINERY '87, Napa Vly., Reserve $23.00	S	B	S	S	B				S
GARY FARRELL WINES '89, Sonoma Co., Ladi's Vnyd. $18.00	B		S			B	B	G	S
HANNA WINERY '88, Sonoma Co. $18.00	S		B	B	B		S	S	
MERIDIAN VINEYARDS '89, Paso Robles $12.00	G	B	S		G	G			B
SIGNORELLO VINEYARDS '89, Napa Vly., Founder's Reserve $25.00	S			S	G		G	G	B
VICHON WINERY '88, Napa Vly., Stag's Leap Dist. $24.00	G	B		S	B	B			B
VILLA MT. EDEN WINERY '88, California, Cellar Select $9.00	G	B	S		S		S	S	
WINDSOR VINEYARDS '88, Sonoma Co., Signature Series $18.00		S		B		B	B	S	S
WINDSOR VINEYARDS '85, Mendocino Co., Haehl Ranch $12.00	G	B	S			B	S		B
5 AWARDS									
BAREFOOT CELLARS 'NV, California $5.00	B	B		S			S		B
BURGESS CELLARS '88, Napa Vly., Vintage Selection $19.00	S	B	B					B	S

Cabernet Sauvignon

5 AWARDS

San Diego	W. Coast	Nat'l O.S.	State Fair	Dallas	San Fran	Farmers	Orange	L.A.	Winery
		G	B	G	B		G		**CASTORO CELLARS** '89, Paso Robles $10.00
S	B		B		B		B		**CHATEAU DE LEU WINERY** '89, Napa Vly. $14.00
S	S		G		S	B			**CHAUFFE-EAU CELLARS** '87, Alexander Vly. $16.00
	G	S			S		B	G	**CLOS DU BOIS** '88, Alexander Vly., Briarcrest $21.00
	B		S		B	S	G		**DE LOACH VINEYARDS** '89, Russian River Vly., Estate $16.00
S		B		B			S	G	**FETZER VINEYARDS** '89, California, Valley Oaks $7.00
	S		S	B			S	B	**FETZER VINEYARDS** '88, California, Barrel Select $11.00
		S	B	B	B			G	**FETZER VINEYARDS** '86, Sonoma Co., Reserve $24.00
B	B	S		B			S		**GRAND CRU VINEYARDS** '88, Sonoma, Prem. Sel. $12.00
	S		B	B		G		G	**HUSCH VINEYARDS** '88, Mendocino, North Field $18.00
			S	G	S		G	S	**KENDALL-JACKSON WINERY** '89, California, Vintner's Reserve $13.00
	G				B	B	S	G	**KENWOOD VINEYARDS** '89, Sonoma, Jack London Vnyd. $20.00
		G	B			S	S	G	**NAVARRO VINEYARDS** '87, Mendocino $16.00
B	B		B			S	S		**RODNEY STRONG VINEYARDS** '89, Sonoma Co. $10.00
B		G		S		B	G		**VILLA MT. EDEN WINERY** '88, Napa Vly., Reserve $12.00
G	B		G		B		S		**VINA VISTA WINERY** '87, Alexander Vly. $16.00
S		S			B		B	G	**WILLIAM WHEELER WINERY** '88, Dry Creek Vly. $15.00

4 AWARDS

San Diego	W. Coast	Nat'l O.S.	State Fair	Dallas	San Fran	Farmers	Orange	L.A.	Winery
	S		B	B			B		**BLACK MOUNTAIN VINEYARD** '88, Alexander Vly., Fat Cat $18.00

Cabernet Sauvignon

	L.A.	Orange	Farmers	San Fran	Dallas	State Fair	Nat'l O.S.	W. Coast	San Diego
4 AWARDS									
CHATOM VINEYARDS '89, Calaveras Co. $14.00		S	B			B			B
CLOS PEGASE WINERY '87, Napa Vly. $18.50	B	S	B			S			
CONN CREEK WINERY '87, Napa Vly. $17.00					B	B	S	B	
CRESTON VINEYARDS '87, Paso Robles, Winemakers Sel. $25.00	S	G				B	B		
GEYSER PEAK WINERY '89, Alexander Vly., Est. Res. $15.00		G		B			B	S	
GRGICH HILLS CELLAR '86, Napa Vly. $20.00	B		B				G		B
GUENOC WINERY '89, Napa Vly., Beckstoffer, Res. $24.00		S		S				S	B
GUGLIELMO WINERY '86, Santa Clara, Reserve $10.00	S		B		S				B
HUSCH VINEYARDS '89, Mendocino, La Ribera $8.00	S	S	S					S	
INGLENOOK-NAPA VALLEY '88, Napa Vly. $9.50	B	S	G				S		
INGLENOOK-NAPA VALLEY '87, Napa Vly., Reserve Cask $17.00	B	S	B	B					
LOCKWOOD VINEYARD '90, Monterey, Partners Res. $16.00	G		B			G			S
PEJU PROVINCE '89, Napa Vly. $14.50		B				B		S	B
PEJU PROVINCE '89, Napa Vly., HB Vnyd. $30.00				G	G	B		S	
R. H. PHILLIPS VINEYARD '90, California $8.00	S	B	B						B
QUIVIRA VINEYARDS '88, Dry Creek Vly. $14.75	B	B			B				B
A. RAFANELLI WINERY '89, Dry Creek Vly. $15.00	G					B		G	S
RICHARDSON VINEYARDS '89, Sonoma Vly., Home $14.00		B	B	B				S	
ROMBAUER VINEYARDS '87, Napa Vly. $15.00		B			G	B	G		

Cabernet Sauvignon

San Diego	W. Coast	Nat'l O.S.	State Fair	Dallas	San Fran	Farmers	Orange	L.A.	Wine
									4 AWARDS
		S	B	S		B			**SEQUOIA GROVE VINEYARDS** '88, Napa Vly. $16.00
		B		B		B		G	**SEQUOIA GROVE VINEYARDS** '88, Napa Vly., Estate $25.00
			G			B	G	S	**VICHON WINERY** '89, Napa Vly., Tenth Harvest $16.00
B	S		S		B				**ZD WINES** '89, Napa Vly. $16.00
									3 AWARDS
	B		B			B			**BANDIERA WINERY** '88, Napa Vly. $6.50
		S	S				G		**BEAULIEU VINEYARD** '87, Napa Co., Geo. De Latou $37.00
	B				B	B			**BERINGER VINEYARDS** '89, Knight's Vly., Proprietor Grown $16.00
B		B		B					**BUENA VISTA WINERY** '88, Cameros, Estate $12.00
			B			S	B		**CHATEAU SOUVERAIN** '88, Alexander Vly. $10.00
G							S	S	**B. R. COHN** '89, Sonoma Vly., Olive Hill Vnyd. $25.00
			B				B	S	**CORBETT CANYON VINEYARDS** '89, California, Coastal Classic $8.00
S	B							S	**COSENTINO WINERY** '88, North Coast, Reserve $27.00
					B	S	B		**CYPRESS** '88, California $7.75
B	S					B			**DEER VALLEY VINEYARDS** '88, California $5.49
S				S			S		**DEHLINGER WINERY** '88, Russian River Vly., Estate $15.00
			S		S			B	**DURNEY VINEYARDS** '90, Carmel Vly., Durney Vnyd. $12.00
G		S		B					**EBERLE WINERY** '88, Paso Robles, Estate $15.00
B		S		B					**ESTANCIA VINEYARDS** '89, Alexander Vly. $9.00

Cabernet Sauvignon

	L.A.	Orange	Farmers	San Fran	Dallas	State Fair	Nat'l O.S.	W. Coast	San Diego
3 AWARDS									
THOMAS FOGARTY WINERY '86, Napa Vly. $15.50			B				B		G
FREEMARK ABBEY '88, Napa Vly. $16.00	B		B			B			
E. & J. GALLO 'NV, California $5.00	S		B				B		
GLEN ELLEN WINERY '89, California, Prop. Reserve $6.00	B	B				S			
GREENWOOD RIDGE VINEYARDS '88, Mendocino, Estate $12.00		S					S		S
GUNDLACH-BUNDSCHU '89, Sonoma Co., Rhinefarm Vnyds. $15.00	B			B		B			
GUSTAVE NIEBAUM COLLECTION '87, Napa Vly., Mast Vnyd. $14.00	S	S		G					
HACIENDA WINERY '86, Sonoma Co. $15.00			G		B				S
HARMONY CELLARS '89, Paso Robles $11.75		S	S					B	
HUSCH VINEYARDS '88, Mendocino, La Ribera Vnyd. $14.00					B			B	B
INDIAN SPRINGS VINEYARDS '88, Sierra Foothills $11.00	S	B						B	
TOBIN JAMES '90, Paso Robles, Private Stash $14.00	B			B				B	
LAMBERT BRIDGE '89, Sonoma Co. $16.00		B		B					S
LAVA CAP WINERY '87, El Dorado, Estate $10.00		S					B	B	
LEEWARD WINERY '88, Alexander Vly. $13.00			S			B		B	
J. LOHR WINERY '89, Paso Robles, Seven Oaks $12.25	G		B	G					
J. LOHR WINERY '88, Paso Robles, Seven Oaks $12.00		B			G			G	
MAACAMA CREEK '89, Sonoma Co., Melim Vnyd. $9.00	G	S				B			
MADRONA VINEYARDS '85, El Dorado, Madrona Vnyd $12.00		S	S				B		

Cabernet Sauvignon

3 AWARDS

San Diego	W. Coast	Nat'l O.S.	State Fair	Dallas	San Fran	Farmers	Orange	L.A.	Winery
G				B			B		**M. MARION** '89, California
S				B			B		**ROBERT MONDAVI WINERY** '88, Napa Vly., Unfiltered, Reserve $40.00
						S	G	S	**NAPA RIDGE** '89, North Coast $7.50
			B			B	S		**NEVADA CITY WINERY** '89, Nevada Co., Sierra Foothill $11.00
B			B				B		**PELLEGRINI FAMILY VINEYARDS** '89, Cloverdale Ranch, Cuvee
G					B			G	**ROBERT PEPI WINERY** '88, Napa Vly., Vine Hill Ranch $18.00
B	B				B				**RAYMOND VINEYARD** '87, Napa Vly., Reserve $26.00
		B					B	B	**SEGHESIO WINERY** '89, Sonoma Co. $10.00
			B		B		S		**SHENANDOAH VINEYARDS** '89, Amador Co. $9.00
	B					B		G	**STONY RIDGE WINERY** '89, Napa Vly., Ltd. Release $9.50
		B			B			S	**SWANSON VINEYARDS** '88, Napa Vly. $23.00
B			B					G	**VILLA ZAPU** '88, Napa Vly. $19.00
		B			S		B		**WHITEHALL LANE WINERY** '88, Napa Vly. $15.00
	B						S	G	**WINDSOR VINEYARDS** '89, Sonoma Co.
	B	B					S		**WINDSOR VINEYARDS** '87, River West Vnyd. $15.00

2 AWARDS

San Diego	W. Coast	Nat'l O.S.	State Fair	Dallas	San Fran	Farmers	Orange	L.A.	Winery
B				G					**ABBEY D'OR** '87, Paso Robles
	B						B		**ADELAIDA CELLARS** '88, Paso Robles $14.50
		B					G		**ARROWOOD VINEYARDS** '88, Sonoma Co.

Cabernet Sauvignon

2 AWARDS

Winery / Wine	L.A.	Orange	Farmers	San Fran	Dallas	State Fair	Nat'l O.S.	W. Coast	San Diego
AUDUBON CELLARS '90, Napa Vly.	G					B			
BEAULIEU VINEYARD '89, Napa Vly., Rutherford, Estate	S	B							
BENZIGER OF GLEN ELLEN '89, Sonoma Mtn., Estate		B		S					
DAVIS BYNUM WINERY '89, Sonoma Co. $11.00	S			B					
CALLAWAY VINEYARD '89, California, America's Cup $12.00		S		S					
MAURICE CARRIE WINERY '90, Temecula $8.00		B	B						
CAYMUS VINEYARDS '89, Napa Vly. $24.00				G		S			
CHALK HILL WINERY '89, Chalk Hill, Estate $13.00						B	B		
CHATEAU POTELLE '88, Alexander Vly. $16.00			B			B			
CLOS PEGASE WINERY '86, Napa Vly. $18.50							G		S
B. R. COHN '89, Napa Co., Silver Label	B	B							
CORBETT CANYON VINEYARDS '89, Alexander Vly., Reserve $9.00		S		B					
COSENTINO WINERY '87, North Coast. Reserve $27.00	S		B						
DEER PARK WINERY '88, Beatty Ranch/Howell Mtn. Res. $24.00		B		S					
EYE OF THE SWAN CELLARS 'NV, California								B	S
FENESTRA WINERY '89, Livermore Vly. $13.00		S		B					
FENESTRA WINERY '88, Monterey, Smith & Hook Vnyd. $15.00		S		B					
GUENOC WINERY '89, Lake Co. $9.00						B			S
GUENOC WINERY '87, Lake Co. $12.00					S				S

Cabernet Sauvignon

2 AWARDS

San Diego	W. Coast	Nat'l O.S.	State Fair	Dallas	San Fran	Farmers	Orange	L.A.	Wine
B					B				**GUENOC WINERY** '86, Lake Co. $12.00
	S	G							**GUNDLACH-BUNDSCHU** '88, Sonoma Vly., Rhinefarm Vnyds. $12.00
							G	G	**GUSTAVE NIEBAUM COLLECTION** '89, Napa Vly., Reference $14.00
		S						G	**GUSTAVE NIEBAUM COLLECTION** '88, Napa Vly., Tench
		G					B		**HOPE FARMS WINERY** '89, Paso Robles
		B		B					**TOBIN JAMES** '89, Paso Robles, Private Stash $14.00
						B	B		**CHARLES KRUG WINERY** '88, Napa Vly., Estate $12.00
		B				B			**LOLONIS WINERY** '89, Mendocino Co., Reserve $16.00
				S				B	**MADDALENA VINEYARD** '88, Sonoma Co. $8.00
						B	B		**PAUL MASSON VINEYARDS** '88, Monterey Co. $7.99
			G		G				**MEEKER VINEYARD** '87, Dry Creek Vly. $14.00
			S					B	**MEEKER VINEYARD** '86, Dry Creek Vly. $14.00
		B		S					**MELIM VINEYARDS** '89, Alex. Vly., Maacama Creek $12.00
	S						B		**MENDOCINO HILLS VINEYARDS** '89, Mendocino Co.
		S					B		**MOCERI CELLARS** '89, Sonoma Co.
				S			B		**ROBERT MONDAVI WINERY** '88, Napa Vly. $18.00
	B				B				**MONTICELLO CELLARS** '89, Napa Vly., Corley Reserve $25.00
	S						S		**MONTICELLO CELLARS** '89, Napa Vly., Jefferson Cuvee $15.00
B				S					**MONTICELLO CELLARS** '88, Napa Vly., Jefferson Cuvee $15.00

Cabernet Sauvignon

Wine	L.A.	Orange	Farmers	San Fran	Dallas	State Fair	Nat'l O.S.	W. Coast	San Diego
2 AWARDS									
J. W. MORRIS WINERY '89, California, Private Reserve $8.00		B			S				
MURPHY-GOODE WINERY '89, Alexander Vly., Murphy Ranch $16.00								B	B
MURPHY-GOODE WINERY '88, Alexander Vly. $16.00	B			B					
PRESTON VINEYARDS '88, Dry Creek Vly. $14.00				S		B			
RANCHO SISQUOC '88, Santa Maria Vly.		S							G
RAYMOND VINEYARD '88, Napa Vly. $15.00				B	B				
RENAISSANCE VINEYARD '87, North Yuba $15.00								B	S
RIVER RUN '89, Mendocino, Mountanos $10.00		G		B					
RUTHERFORD RANCH '87, Napa Vly. $15.00						B	S		
V. SATTUI WINERY '87, Napa Vly. $14.00					S				S
SEBASTIANI VINEYARDS '88, Sonoma Co.						B			B
SOBON ESTATE '88, Amador Co.	S							S	
ST. CLEMENT VINEYARDS '89, Napa Vly. $20.00	B					B			
ST. CLEMENT VINEYARDS '88, Napa Vly. $20.00				S			S		
STAG'S LEAP WINE CELLARS '89, Napa Vly., SLV/Fay Vnyd. $27.00			B	S					
STONE CREEK CELLARS '86, Napa Vly., Special Selection						S			S
J. STONESTREET & SONS '88, Alexander Vly. $24.00		G		S					
STONY RIDGE WINERY '89, California	S						S		
RODNEY STRONG VINEYARDS '88, Alexander's Crown $17.00	G					G			

Cabernet Sauvignon

2 AWARDS

San Diego	W. Coast	Nat'l O.S.	State Fair	Dallas	San Fran	Farmers	Orange	L.A.	Winery
		S		S					**RODNEY STRONG VINEYARDS** '87, Alexander's Crown $17.00
		B					B		**TREFETHEN VINEYARDS** '87, Napa, Trefethen Vnyd. $16.00
B							B		**TULOCAY WINERY** '87, Napa Vly., Cliff Vnyd.
	B						S		**TWIN HILLS RANCH WINERY** '88, Paso Robles, Estate
					S			B	**M. G. VALLEJO WINERY** '89, California $5.99
B						S			**VALLEY OF THE MOON WINERY** '88, Sonoma Co., Reserve $9.00
							B	S	**WILD HORSE WINERY** '89, Paso Robles $13.00
					B		G		**J. WILE & SONS** '87, Napa Vly. $10.00

CHALK HILL
1990 ESTATE BOTTLED
CHARDONNAY
CHALK HILL, SONOMA COUNTY
Frederick P. Furth, Proprietor

ST. SUPERY
Chardonnay
NAPA VALLEY
Grown, produced and bottled by
8440 St. Helena Highway, Ruther
FINE WHITE

Chardonnay

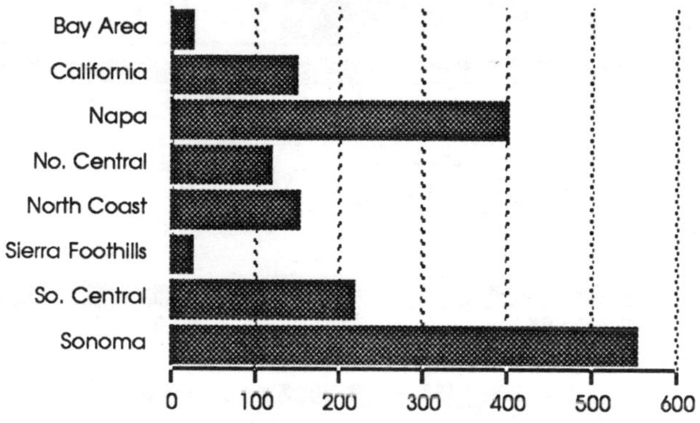

Regional Comparison of Total Points

(Gold=5 Silver=3 Bronze=1)

Highest individual wine totals

24	**ST. SUPERY WINERY** '90, Napa Vly., Dollarhide Ranch $13.00
24	**CHALK HILL WINERY** '90, Sonoma Co., Chalk Hill, Estate $15.00
20	**ST. CLEMENT VINEYARDS** '90, Napa Vly. $16.00
19	**HIDDEN CELLARS** '90, Mendocino Co. $12.00
18	**CHATEAU DE BAUN WINERY** '90, Russian River Vly., Barrel Ferm. $10.00
17	**BELVEDERE WINERY** '90, Russian River Vly. $13.00
16	**KENDALL-JACKSON WINERY** '90, Calif., Prop. Grand Reserve $22.50
16	**LAVA CAP WINERY** '90, El Dorado, Estate, Reserve $14.00
16	**SANTA BARBARA WINERY** '90, Santa Barbara, Reserve $20.00
16	**ROCHIOLI VINEYARD** '90, Russian River Vly., Estate $14.00
16	**J. STONESTREET & SONS** '90, Sonoma Co. $20.00

Chardonnay	L.A.	Orange	Farmers	San Fran	Dallas	State Fair	Nat'l O.S.	W. Coast	San Diego
8 AWARDS									
CHALK HILL WINERY '90, Sonoma Co., Chalk Hill, Estate $15.00	G	B	B	G	B	G		G	B
CHATEAU DE BAUN WINERY '90, Russian River Vly., Barrel Ferm. $10.00	B	B	B	B	S	B		G	G
ST. CLEMENT VINEYARDS '90, Napa Vly. $16.00		B	B	G	B	B	G	S	S
7 AWARDS									
VICHON WINERY '90, Napa Vly. $15.00	B		B	B	S	B		B	S
6 AWARDS									
DE LOACH VINEYARDS '90, Russian River Vly. $15.00	G		S		B	B		B	B
GABRIELLI WINERY '90, Mendocino $16.00		S	B			B	B	B	G
HUSCH VINEYARDS '90, Mendocino, Estate $12.00	B	B		B	B	B		B	
LAVA CAP WINERY '90, El Dorado, Estate, Reserve $14.00		B	S	B		G		B	G
MIRASSOU VINEYARDS '90, Monterey, 5th Gen., Harvest Res. $12.50	G	B	B	S				S	B
ROCHIOLI VINEYARD '90, Russian River Vly., Estate $14.00	S	B	S			S		B	G
ST. SUPERY WINERY '90, Napa Vly., Dollarhide Ranch $13.00		B	G	G	G			S	G
J. STONESTREET & SONS '90, Sonoma Co. $20.00	G	G	B	B		S		B	
WINDSOR VINEYARDS '90, Sonoma Co., Signature Series $20.00	S		B	B		B	S		G
5 AWARDS									
BELVEDERE WINERY '90, Russian River Vly. $13.00		S	B	G		S		G	
BENZIGER OF GLEN ELLEN '90, Sonoma Co. $12.00		G	S	B	S				S
BERINGER VINEYARDS '90, Napa Vly., Prop Grown, Reserve $19.00		B	B	S	G		G		
BERINGER VINEYARDS '90, Napa Vly., Prop. Grown $12.00	G	B			B	S			B

Chardonnay

San Diego	W. Coast	Nat'l O.S.	State Fair	Dallas	San Fran	Farmers	Orange	L.A.	Chardonnay
									5 AWARDS
	S		B		B		G	S	**BYRON VINEYARD** '90, Santa Barbara Co. $14.00
B	B				B		B	S	**FETZER VINEYARDS** '91, California, Sundial $7.00
B	S	B			B	S			**GOOSECROSS CELLARS** '89, Napa Vly., Estate $11.99
B	G					G	S	G	**HIDDEN CELLARS** '90, Mendocino Co. $12.00
B			B			S	S	B	**KENDALL-JACKSON WINERY** '91, California, Vintner's Reserve $13.00
B	S		S		B	B			**KENDALL-JACKSON WINERY** '90, Sonoma Vly., Durell Vnyd. $16.00
S				S	B	B		S	**LANDMARK VINEYARDS** '90, Sonoma Co. $12.00
G			B		B	G		B	**LOCKWOOD VINEYARD** '90, Monterey, Partners Reserve $13.00
	B		B			G	B	B	**MC ILROY WINES** '90, Russian River Vly. $15.50
S	S	G					B	B	**SIGNORELLO VINEYARDS** '90, Napa Vly., Estate $18.00
B		B		S			B	G	**ST. CLEMENT VINEYARDS** '90, Carneros Abbotts Vnyd. $18.00
			B	B		S	S	B	**RODNEY STRONG VINEYARDS** '90, Sonoma Co., Chalk Hill Vnyd. $13.00
B	B				S		S	B	**TAFT STREET WINERY** '90, Sonoma Co. $8.00
B	S					S	B	S	**VINA VISTA WINERY** '89, Alexander Vly., Wasson Vnyd. $10.00
									4 AWARDS
	B				S		B	B	**BARGETTO WINERY** '90, Central Coast, Cypress $9.00
B				B		B	B		**BEAULIEU VINEYARD** '89, Napa Vly., Carneros Reserve $17.00
	S		S	B	B				**BELVEDERE WINERY** '90, Sonoma Co., Preferred Stock $18.00
B	S						B	S	**BOGLE VINEYARDS** '91, California $6.00

Chardonnay

	L.A.	Orange	Farmers	San Fran	Dallas	State Fair	Nat'l O.S.	W. Coast	San Diego
4 AWARDS									
CAMBRIA WINERY '89, Santa Maria Vly., Reserve $25.00			S		B			G	S
CANYON ROAD CELLARS '91, California $4.00	S			B		S		B	
CASTORO CELLARS '91, San Luis Obispo Co. $9.50		G	G			B			S
DRY CREEK VINEYARD '90, Sonoma Co. $13.25		B		B				B	B
ESTANCIA VINEYARDS '90, Monterey $9.00		S	B		B				B
FISHER VINEYARDS '89, Sonoma Co., Coach Insignia $15.00	S	S		B	S				
FRANCISCAN OAKVILLE ESTATE '90, Napa Vly. $12.00			B	B		B		S	
FRANCISCAN OAKVILLE ESTATE '90, Napa Vly., Cuvee Sauvage $24.00		S					S	B	G
GAINEY VINEYARD '90, Santa Barbara Co. $13.00	S	G				B		B	
GEYSER PEAK WINERY '90, Sonoma Co. $8.00			B		B			S	S
GIRARD WINERY '90, Napa Vly., Estate $16.00		B	B	S	B				
HANDLEY CELLARS '90, Dry Creek Vly. $14.50			B		B		B	B	
KENDALL-JACKSON WINERY '90, California, Prop. Grand Reserve $22.50	G	S	S	G					
LOLONIS WINERY '90, Mendocino Co., Reserve $19.00		G		B	B				B
ROBERT MONDAVI WINERY '90, Napa Vly., Reserve $26.00		B			B		S		B
NAVARRO VINEYARDS '90, Anderson Vly., Reserve $14.00	B	G	S			S			
R. H. PHILLIPS VINEYARD '91, California, Barrel Cuvee $8.00	S		S					S	B
RAYMOND VINEYARD '90, Napa Vly. $11.00	S			B		S		B	
SANTA BARBARA WINERY '90, Santa Barbara Co. $12.00	S			B	B	B			

Chardonnay

San Diego	W. Coast	Nat'l O.S.	State Fair	Dallas	San Fran	Farmers	Orange	L.A.	Chardonnay
									4 AWARDS
	S		S		G			G	**SANTA BARBARA WINERY** '90, Santa Barbara, Reserve $20.00
S			B	S		B			**SONOMA CREEK WINERY** '90, Carneros, Barrel Ferm. $12.00
	B					B	B	B	**VILLA MT. EDEN WINERY** '90, California, Select $9.00
B		B					B	S	**WHITE OAK VINEYARDS** '90, Sonoma Co., Myers Reserve $20.00
	B	B					G	S	**WINDSOR VINEYARDS** '89, Sonoma Co., Reserve $13.00
G	G					B		B	**ZACA MESA WINERY** '89, Santa Barbara Co., Reserve $16.50
									3 AWARDS
		B			B	S			**ARCIERO WINERY** '89, Paso Robles, Estate $8.69
B				B	G				**BARGETTO WINERY** '90, Santa Cruz Mtns. $18.00
		G			B	B			**BLACK MOUNTAIN VINEYARD** '88, Alexander Vly., Gravel Bar $18.00
S						B		S	**BUENA VISTA WINERY** '90, Carneros $11.00
	B	G				B			**BUENA VISTA WINERY** '89, Carneros, Reserve $17.50
			S			B		S	**CAMBRIA WINERY** '90, Santa Maria, Katherine's Vnyd. $16.00
						B	B	S	**CHATEAU JULIEN WINERY** '90, Monterey Co., Sur Lie, Reserve $15.00
	G					S	B		**CHAUFFE-EAU CELLARS** '90, Carneros, Sangiacomo $16.00
			B		B		B		**CLOS DU BOIS** '90, Dry Creek Vly., Flintwood $17.00
G		S				B			**CLOS PEGASE WINERY** '88, Los Carneros $16.50
G					B	B			**CONCANNON VINEYARD** '88, Santa Clara Vly., Mistral Vnyd. $11.75
B	S						B		**DE LORIMIER WINERY** '90, Alexander Vly., Estate, Prism $15.00

Chardonnay

3 AWARDS	L.A.	Orange	Farmers	San Fran	Dallas	State Fair	Nat'l O.S.	W. Coast	San Diego
DEHLINGER WINERY '90, Russian River Vly., Estate $13.00		S				B		S	
DOMAINE MICHEL '89, Sonoma Co. $15.00			B	B		B			
DREYER SONOMA WINERY '90, Carneros $15.00		S	S						B
DRY CREEK VINEYARD '88, Sonoma Co., Reserve $20.00			S				G	B	
GARY FARRELL WINES '90, Russian River Vly. $18.00		S			B				S
FIRESTONE VINEYARD '90, Santa Ynez Vly., Barrel Ferm. $12.00				B		B			B
FREEMARK ABBEY '90, Napa Vly., Carpy Ranch $22.00	S	G				B			
GOOSECROSS CELLARS '89, Napa Vly. $8.99	B		B			S			
GRAND CRU VINEYARDS '89, Carneros, Premium Selection $13.50							S	B	B
GREENWOOD RIDGE VINEYARDS '90, Mendocino $16.00			S				G	S	
GUENOC WINERY '90, Guenoc Vly., Barrel Ferm. $14.00	G	B						S	
GUENOC WINERY '90, Guenoc Vly., Magoon Vnyd.. Res. $23.00		B		S		S			
GUNDLACH-BUNDSCHU '90, Sonoma Vly., Estate $12.00		B		B	B				
GUSTAVE NIEBAUM COLLECTION '89, Carneros, Bayview Vnyd. $13.50		B	S						B
HANDLEY CELLARS '89, Anderson Vly. $11.00			S		B			G	
HANNA WINERY '90, Sonoma Co. $14.00						B	B		B
HAYWOOD WINERY '90, California, Vintners Select $8.00	S	B	B						
HIDDEN CELLARS '90, Mendocino Co., Reserve $16.00		S			B		B		

Chardonnay

San Diego	W. Coast	Nat'l O.S.	State Fair	Dallas	San Fran	Farmers	Orange	L.A.	3 AWARDS
					S		B	S	**LAMBERT BRIDGE** '90, Sonoma Co. $14.00
					S	G		B	**LAURIER** '89, Sonoma Co. $15.00
B			B				B		**LAVA CAP WINERY** '90, El Dorado $10.00
S			S			G			**LEEWARD WINERY** '90, Central Coast $11.00
B						S	B		**LEEWARD WINERY** '90, Monterey $14.00
S		B				B			**LOCKWOOD VINEYARD** '90, Monterey, Estate $7.50
	B		B					S	**MAZZOCCO VINEYARDS** '89, Alexander Vly. $16.00
B			B			S			**MERIDIAN VINEYARDS** '90, Edna Vly. $15.00
		S				B		B	**MERIDIAN VINEYARDS** '90, Santa Barbara Co. $10.00
	S			B	B				**RABBIT RIDGE VINEYARDS** '90, Russian River, Rabbit Ridge Ranch $12.00
	G		S		S				**KENT RASMUSSEN WINERY** '90, Napa Vly. $17.00
		S		B		G			**V. SATTUI WINERY** '90, Napa Vly., Carsi Vinyd., Estate $15.00
B			B				S		**SEBASTIANI VINEYARDS** '90, Sonoma Co., Family Selection
	B				S	S			**SEQUOIA GROVE VINEYARDS** '89, Napa Vly., Carneros $14.00
S						B	S		**STAG'S LEAP WINE CELLARS** '90, Napa Vly. $18.75
				B	B		B		**STORRS WINERY** '90, Santa Cruz Mtns. $20.00
B				B			S		**RODNEY STRONG VINEYARDS** '90, Sonoma Co. $9.00
B		B	B						**WILLIAM WHEELER WINERY** '90, Sonoma Co. $13.00

Chardonnay

Chardonnay	L.A.	Orange	Farmers	San Fran	Dallas	State Fair	Nat'l O.S.	W. Coast	San Diego
3 AWARDS									
ZACA MESA WINERY '90, Santa Barbara Co. $11.00		B	B					G	
ZD WINES '90, California $20.00		G			B		B		
2 AWARDS									
ACACIA '90, Napa Vly., Carneros	S	B							
ADELAIDA CELLARS '90, Paso Robles	S	S							
ALDERBROOK WINERY '90, Dry Creek Vly. $11.00				B		B			
ANGELS CREEK '88, California		B						B	
ARMIDA WINERY '90, Russian River Vly.		G			B				
BAREFOOT CELLARS 'NV, California $5.00	S								S
BENZIGER OF GLEN ELLEN '90, Carneros, Premiere Vnyd.		S							S
BOUCHAINE VINEYARDS '90, Napa Vly. $15.00		B	S						
BYRON VINEYARD '90, Santa Barbara Co., Reserve $18.00		G		G					
CARNEROS CREEK WINERY '90, Los Carneros $12.50					B				B
MAURICE CARRIE WINERY '89, Temecula $7.50			B					B	
CASK ONE '90, Mendocino		S				B			
CHANDELLE OF SONOMA '90, Sonoma Co., Chandelle Vnyd. $8.00				B	G				
CHAPPELLET VINEYARD '89, Napa Vly. $14.00			B	S					
CHATEAU DE LEU WINERY '90, Solano Co., Green Vly. $14.00						B		S	
CHATEAU SOUVERAIN '88, Carneros, Reserve $14.00								B	B

Chardonnay

San Diego	W. Coast	Nat'l O.S.	State Fair	Dallas	San Fran	Farmers	Orange	L.A.	
									2 AWARDS
S							B		**CHATEAU ST. JEAN** '90, Sonoma Vly., Estate Selection
				B	S				**CHATEAU ST. JEAN** '89, Alexander Vly., Belle Terre $18.00
		S					G		**CLONINGER CELLARS** '89, Monterey Co.
			S		G				**CLOS DU BOIS** '91, Alexander Vly. $12.00
		S				B			**CLOS DU MURIEL** '89, California $7.00
B	B								**CLOS PEGASE WINERY** '89, Napa Vly. $12.00
	B						B		**CORBETT CANYON VINEYARDS** '91, Central Coast, Coastal Classic $8.00
B								B	**COSENTINO WINERY** '90, Napa Vly., The Sculptor
B	B								**CRESTON VINEYARDS** '89, Paso Robles, Barrel Ferm.
				B			S		**CRICHTON HALL** '90, Napa Vly., Chardonnay Vnyd.
					B		S		**DE LOACH VINEYARDS** '90, Russian River Vly., O.F.S. $25.00
				S		B			**DOMAINE BRETON** '90, California $8.00
B						B			**DOMAINE BRETON** '89, California $8.00
		G					S		**DOMAINE DE CLARCK** '90, Monterey Co., Reserve
		B				S			**DOMAINE NAPA WINERY** '89, Napa Vly. $12.50
B							B		**DRY CREEK VINEYARD** '90, Dry Creek Vly., Reserve $20.00
	B						B		**DUNNEWOOD VINEYARDS** '90, North Coast, Barrel Select
						B	B		**FENESTRA WINERY** '90, Livermore Vly. $12.50
	B		G						**FETZER VINEYARDS** '90, Mendocino Co. $20.00

Chardonnay

	L.A.	Orange	Farmers	San Fran	Dallas	State Fair	Nat'l O.S.	W. Coast	San Diego
2 AWARDS									
FETZER VINEYARDS '90, Mendocino Co., Barrel Select $11.00		B						S	
FOLIE A DEUX WINERY '90, Napa Vly. $16.50	B	B							
GLEN ELLEN WINERY '91, California, Prop. Reserve. $6.00	B	B							
GOLD HILL VINEYARD '89, El Dorado Co. $10.00								B	S
GRGICH HILLS CELLAR '89, Napa Vly. $22.00			G						G
GROTH VINEYARDS '90, Napa Vly. $14.00		S		B					
GUENOC WINERY '90, California $8.50		B	B						
GUSTAVE NIEBAUM COLLECTION '89, Napa Vly., Carneros, Laird Vnyd. $12.50			G						B
HAHN ESTATES '90, Monterey, Santa Lucia Highlands $9.00				S				B	
HART WINERY '90, Temecula $12.00		B	S						
HAYWOOD WINERY '89, Sonoma, Los Chamizal Vnyd. $14.00		B	B						
HUSCH VINEYARDS '89, Anderson Vly., Estate, Reserve $18.00			B	B					
JEKEL VINEYARDS '90, Arroyo Seco, Estate $11.95			S	B					
KENDALL-JACKSON WINERY '90, California, Vintner's Reserve $13.00					B		B		
KONOCTI WINERY '90, Lake Co. $10.00					B				B
LANDMARK VINEYARDS '90, Alex. Vly., Damaris Vnyd., Res. $16.00				B	S				
LEEWARD WINERY '90, Edna Vly. $15.00		B							B
LOCKWOOD VINEYARD '89, Monterey Co., Estate $13.00			B						B
MADDALENA VINEYARD '90, Central Coast $8.00	B	B							

Chardonnay

2 AWARDS

San Diego	W. Coast	Nat'l O.S.	State Fair	Dallas	San Fran	Farmers	Orange	L.A.	Chardonnay
							B	S	**MARK WEST VINEYARDS** '90, Russian River, La Beau Vnyd. $12.50
B							B		**MARTINELLI VINEYARDS** '90, Russian River Vly., Estate $10.00
		S					S		**LOUIS M. MARTINI WINERY** '90, Sonoma Co./Napa Co. $8.00
S							S		**MATANZAS CREEK WINERY** '90, Sonoma Vly. $19.00
				B			B		**MERRYVALE VINEYARDS** '90, Napa Vly., Starmont
S			B						**MIRASSOU VINEYARDS** '90, Monterey Co., Family Selection $9.75
				B			S		**MORGAN** '90, Monterey
			B				G		**MOUNT PALOMAR WINERY** '91, Temecula $10.00
B							S		**MOUNT PALOMAR WINERY** '91, Temecula, Reserve $16.00
		S	B						**NAPA CREEK** '90, Napa Vly. $15.00
		S						B	**NAPA CREEK** '89, Napa Vly. $15.00
						S	B		**J. PEDRONCELLI WINERY** '90, Dry Creek Vly. $9.50
G						B			**RAYMOND VINEYARD** '90, Napa Vly., Reserve $18.00
B						B			**REVERE VINEYARD** '88, Napa Vly. $14.00
B					B				**ROUND HILL CELLARS** '90, Napa Vly., Reserve $11.00
		G					B		**ROYCE VINEYARDS** '90, California
		B					S		**SANFORD WINERY** '90, Santa Barbara Co., Barrel Sel. $28.00
S							B		**SEBASTIANI VINEYARDS** '90, Sonoma Co., Family Sel., Reserve
S				B					**SEQUOIA GROVE VINEYARDS** '90, Napa Vly., Carneros $14.00

Chardonnay

Chardonnay	L.A.	Orange	Farmers	San Fran	Dallas	State Fair	Nat'l O.S.	W. Coast	San Diego
2 AWARDS									
SEQUOIA GROVE VINEYARDS '89, Napa Vly., Allen Fam., Estate $16.00	B					B			
SHAFER VINEYARDS '90, Napa Vly. $15.00		B						S	
ST. FRANCIS WINERY '90, Sonoma Co. $10.00			B				B		
STAGLIN FAMILY VINEYARDS '90, Napa Vly. $20.00				B		B			
STERLING VINEYARDS '88, Napa, Diamond Mtn. Ranch $16.00			B						B
STONY RIDGE WINERY '91, Sonoma Co.	B					B			
TROUT GULCH VINEYARDS '90, Santa Cruz Mtns.		G				B			
TULOCAY WINERY '89, Napa Vly., De Celles Vnyd.								B	B
M. G. VALLEJO WINERY '90, California $5.99					B				B
VICHON WINERY '89, Napa Vly. $16.00				S			G		
WENTE BROS. '90, Central Coast $8.00	B		B						
WHITE OAK VINEYARDS '91, Sonoma Co. $12.95	B					S			
WILDHURST VINEYARDS '90, Napa Vly.						S			B
WINDMERE WINES '90, Edna Vly., MacGregor Vnyd. $13.50		B						B	

Dry Creek Vineyard
DRY CHENIN BLANC
California
1 9 9 1

Chenin Blanc

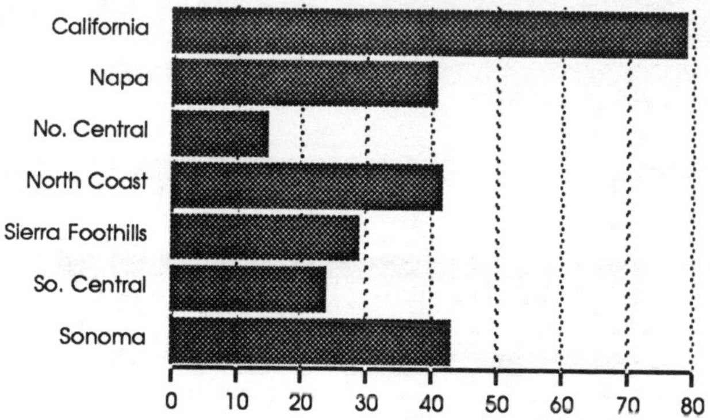

Regional Comparison of Total Points

(Gold=5 Silver=3 Bronze=1)

Highest individual wine totals

25	**DRY CREEK VINEYARD** '91, California $7.00
19	**R. H. PHILLIPS VINEYARD** '91, California, Dry $5.00
18	**FETZER VINEYARDS** '90, Mendocino Co. $6.00
18	**PARDUCCI WINE CELLARS** '91, Mendocino Co. $6.00
17	**GEYSER PEAK WINERY** '91, Alexander Vly., Soft $5.50
14	**GRAND CRU VINEYARDS** '91, Clarksburg $7.00
14	**WINDSOR VINEYARDS** '91, Sonoma Co. $6.50
13	**MAURICE CARRIE WINERY** '90, Temecula, Estate, Soft $5.00
11	**GUENOC WINERY** '90, California $6.00
9	**HACIENDA WINERY** '91, Clarksburg, Dry $6.50
7	**LA TOURNELLE** '90, Monterey, Ventana Vnyd. $5.00
7	**WENTE BROS.** '90, Central Coast LeBlanc De Blancs $5.00

Chenin Blanc

Wine	L.A.	Orange	Farmers	San Fran	Dallas	State Fair	Nat'l O.S.	W. Coast	San Diego
9 AWARDS									
DRY CREEK VINEYARD '91, California $7.00	B	G	G	B	B	G	B	S	S
8 AWARDS									
WINDSOR VINEYARDS '91, Sonoma Co. $6.50	B	S	B	B		S	S	B	B
7 AWARDS									
R. H. PHILLIPS VINEYARD '91, California, Dry $5.00	S	G	B	B		G		S	B
5 AWARDS									
GEYSER PEAK WINERY '91, Alexander Vly., Soft $5.50		S	S			G	S		S
GUENOC WINERY '90, California $6.00		S	B				G	B	B
LA TOURNELLE '90, Monterey, Ventana Vnyd. $5.00		B	B	B			S		B
WENTE BROS. '90, Central Coast LeBlanc De Blancs $5.00	S	B	B		B		B		
4 AWARDS									
FETZER VINEYARDS '90, Mendocino Co. $6.00	G					S	G	G	
GRAND CRU VINEYARDS '91, Clarksburg $7.00		G	S				B	G	
PARDUCCI WINE CELLARS '91, Mendocino Co. $6.00	G	G	S			G			
3 AWARDS									
BERINGER VINEYARDS '91, Napa Vly. $7.50			B			B		B	
MAURICE CARRIE WINERY '90, Temecula, Estate, Soft $5.00		G			S				G
CHAPPELLET VINEYARD '89, Napa Vly. $7.50		B	S					B	
DE MOOR WINERY '91, Napa Vly. $6.75			S			B			B
FOLIE A DEUX WINERY '91, Napa Vly. $8.00		B	B	B					
HACIENDA WINERY '91, Clarksburg, Dry $6.50		B				G		S	

Chenin Blanc

San Diego	W. Coast	Nat'l O S.	State Fair	Dallas	San Fran	Farmers	Orange	L.A.	Wine
									3 AWARDS
	S				B		B		**KENWOOD VINEYARDS** '91, California $7.00
B		B				B			**MILAT VINEYARDS** '91, Napa Vly. Estate $6.95
	B			B			S		**PINE RIDGE WINERY** '91, Napa Vly., Yountville Cuvee $8.00
			B	B			S		**SIMI WINERY** '90, Mendocino Co. $6.50
									2 AWARDS
B							S		**ALEXANDER VALLEY VINEYARDS** '90, Alexander Vly., Wetzel Vnyd.
				G				B	**BERINGER VINEYARDS** '90, Napa Vly. $6.00
					B	B			**CALLAWAY VINEYARD** '90, Temecula, Morning Harvest $7.00
				S			B		**EMERALD BAY** '91, California, Prop. Reserve
	B						B		**GOLD HILL VINEYARD** '90, El Dorado $7.00
S		B							**QUINTA DO COTTA** '90, Lodi, Vinho Bianco
		B				B			**WHITE OAK VINEYARDS** '90, Alexander Vly. $6.95

TF

Thomas Fogarty

1991

VENTANA VINEYARDS
MONTEREY

Gewurztraminer

PRODUCED AND BOTTLED BY
THOMAS FOGARTY WINERY, PORTOLA VALLEY, CALIFORNIA
ALCOHOL 12% BY VOLUME CONTAINS SULFITES

1991

LAWRENCE J. BARGETTO

MONTEREY COUNTY / PINNACLES VINEYARD

Dry · Gewurztraminer

PRODUCED AND BOTTLED BY BARGETTO WINERY, SOQUEL, CALIFORNIA, USA ALC. 12% BY VOL.

Gewurztraminer

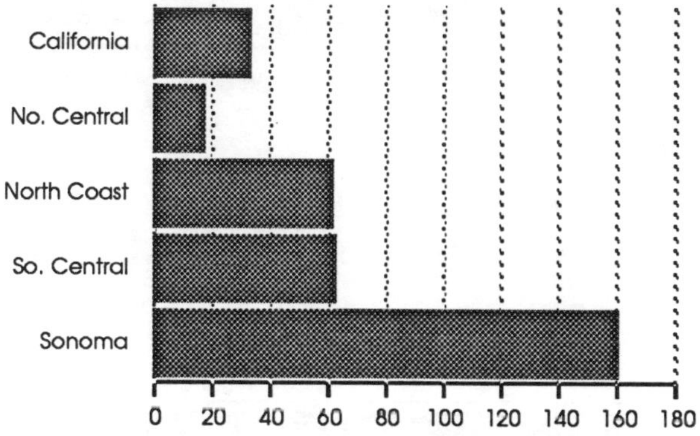

Regional Comparison of Total Points

(Gold=5 Silver=3 Bronze=1)

Highest individual wine totals

29 **THOMAS FOGARTY WINERY**
'91, Monterey, Ventana Vnyds. $10.00

18 **ADLER FELS WINERY**
'91, Sonoma Co. $9.00

15 **BARGETTO WINERY**
'91, Monterey Co. $8.00

14 **NAPA RIDGE**
'90, Central Coast $5.50

13 **KENDALL-JACKSON WINERY**
'91, California, Vintner's Reserve $9.00

13 **HANDLEY CELLARS**
'91, Anderson Vly. $8.00

13 **CHATEAU ST. JEAN**
'90, Alexander Vly., Belle Terre, SLH $15.00

12 **FIRESTONE VINEYARD**
'91, Santa Ynez Vly.

11 **FETZER VINEYARDS**
'91, California $6.00

11 **DE LOACH VINEYARDS**
'91, Russian River, LH $14.00

Gewurztraminer

0 - 3.0 Residual Sugar

Winery	L.A.	Orange	Farmers	San Fran	Dallas	State Fair	Nat'l O.S.	W. Coast	San Diego
7 AWARDS									
THOMAS FOGARTY WINERY '91, Monterey, Ventana Vnyds. $10.00	G	G	G	B		G		G	S
KENDALL-JACKSON WINERY '91, California, Vintner's Reserve $9.00	G	B	B	B		B		S	B
6 AWARDS									
ADLER FELS WINERY '91, Sonoma Co. $9.00	B		G	S		S		S	S
NAPA RIDGE '90, Central Coast $5.50	G	B	B		B	S			S
5 AWARDS									
BARGETTO WINERY '91, Monterey Co. $8.00	S	S			S			B	G
FETZER VINEYARDS '91, California $6.00	S	S		S				B	B
HANDLEY CELLARS '91, Anderson Vly. $8.00	S		B		S			S	S
ST. FRANCIS WINERY '91, Sonoma Co. $7.50	B	S	S	B				B	
WINDSOR VINEYARDS '91, Alexander Vly. $7.50		B	B	B		B			S
4 AWARDS									
DAVIS BYNUM WINERY '91, Russian River $8.00					S	S		S	B
DE LOACH VINEYARDS '91, Russian River Vly., Estate $8.50		S	B				S	B	
FIRESTONE VINEYARD '91, Santa Ynez Vly.	B	S				S		G	
HUSCH VINEYARDS '91, Anderson Vly., Estate $8.50		S	B			S		S	
STONE CREEK CELLARS '90, Sonoma Co., Special Sel.		S			B		B		B
3 AWARDS									
BUENA VISTA WINERY '91, Carneros $7.50		B	S					B	
GEYSER PEAK WINERY '91, California, Soft $5.50		S			B		S		
HUSCH VINEYARDS '90, Anderson Vly., Estate $8.50					S		S	B	

Gewurztraminer
0 - 3.0 Residual Sugar

San Diego	W. Coast	Nat'l O.S.	State Fair	Dallas	San Fran	Farmers	Orange	L.A.	Winery
									3 AWARDS
			G			B		S	**NAVARRO VINEYARDS** '90, Anderson Vly. (dry) $8.50
			B		B			S	**PESENTI WINERY** 'NV, San Luis Obispo Co. $7.00
B							S	B	**QUAFF** '91, Sonoma Co. $7.00
									2 AWARDS
				G	B				**ADLER FELS WINERY** '90, Sonoma Co., Estate $9.00
G							G		**ALEXANDER VALLEY VINEYARDS** '91, Alexander Vly., Wetzel Vnyd.
S						S			**BERINGER VINEYARDS** '91, North Coast $7.50
S				B					**BOUCHAINE VINEYARDS** '90, Russian River Vly., Dry $8.50
B						B			**HOP KILN WINERY** '91, Russian River, M. Griffin Vnyd. $7.50
		B					G		**MARTINELLI VINEYARDS** '91, Russian River Vly., Estate
	S	S							**MILL CREEK VINEYARDS** '91, Dry Creek Vly.
			B				G		**PARDUCCI WINE CELLARS** '91, Mendocino $6.00

Gewurztraminer
3.1 + Residual Sugar

San Diego	W. Coast	Nat'l O.S.	State Fair	Dallas	San Fran	Farmers	Orange	L.A.	Winery
									5 AWARDS
B			B		S	S		S	**DE LOACH VINEYARDS** '91, Russian River, LH, R.S. 13.5 $14.00
									3 AWARDS
					G		S	G	**CHATEAU ST. JEAN** '90, Alexander Vly., Belle Terre Vnyd., SLH, R.S. 15.0 $15.00
	S				B		G		**MARK WEST VINEYARDS** '91, Creekside Vnyd., LH, R.S. 12.0 $13.00

Johannisberg Riesling

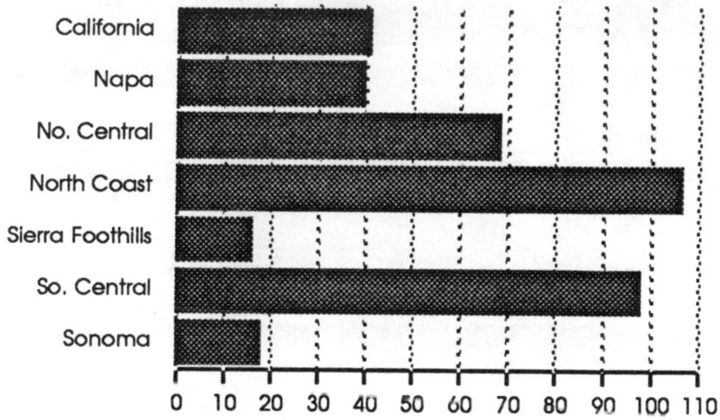

Regional Comparison of Total Points

(Gold=5 Silver=3 Bronze=1)

Highest individual wine totals

20	**FETZER VINEYARDS** '91, California $6.00
17	**V. SATTUI WINERY** '91, Napa Vly. $9.00
15	**MOUNT PALOMAR WINERY** '91, Temecula $6.00
13	**NAVARRO VINEYARDS** '90, Mendocino, LH $12.00
13	**NAVARRO VINEYARDS** '90, Mendocino, CSLH $25.00
13	**FIRESTONE VINEYARD** '91, Santa Ynez Vly. $7.50
11	**AUSTIN CELLARS** '90, Santa Barbara Co. $7.50
10	**HARMONY CELLARS** '91, Paso Robles $8.00
9	**V. SATTUI WINERY** '91, Napa Vly., Off Dry $9.25
9	**KONOCTI WINERY** '89, Lake Co., White Riesling $7.50
9	**WINDSOR VINEYARDS** '91, North Coast $7.00
9	**GAINEY VINEYARD** '91, Santa Ynez Vly. $8.00

Johannisberg Riesling

0 - 3.0 Residual Sugar

Winery	L.A.	Orange	Farmers	San Fran	Dallas	State Fair	Nat'l O.S.	W. Coast	San Diego
6 AWARDS									
FETZER VINEYARDS '91, California $6.00	G			S	S	G		S	B
5 AWARDS									
GAINEY VINEYARD '91, Santa Ynez Vly. $8.00	B	B	S	B		S			
V. SATTUI WINERY '91, Napa Vly. $9.00	S			S		B		G	G
4 AWARDS									
GEYSER PEAK WINERY '91, California, Soft $5.50			B		S	S			B
HARMONY CELLARS '91, Paso Robles $8.00			S			S	S		B
LOCKWOOD VINEYARD '91, Monterey, Lockwood Vnyd. Estate					B	B	B	G	
3 AWARDS									
BAILY VINEYARD '91, Temecula, Wickets Vnyd. $7.95			B	B			B		
BERINGER VINEYARDS '90, North Coast $7.50		S	B		S				
BUTTERFLY CREEK WINERY '90, Sierra Foothills, White Riesling $9.50		S					S		B
FIRESTONE VINEYARD '91, Santa Ynez Vly. $7.50		S				G		G	
KONOCTI WINERY '89, Lake Co., White Riesling $7.50		S	B					G	
V. SATTUI WINERY '91, Napa Vly., Off Dry $9.25	B		G						S
STONY RIDGE WINERY '90, Arroyo Seco, Limited $5.50		S	B					S	
WINDSOR VINEYARDS '91, North Coast $7.00			S	S					S
2 AWARDS									
CALLAWAY VINEYARD '91, Temecula, Seasonal Refuge $7.00		B		S					
FILSINGER VINEYARDS '91, Temecula $6.00	B	S							
FREEMARK ABBEY '91, Napa Vly. $8.50		S	B						

Johannisberg Riesling

0 - 3.0 Residual Sugar

2 AWARDS

San Diego	W. Coast	Nat'l O.S.	State Fair	Dallas	San Fran	Farmers	Orange	L.A.	Wine
						B	G		**GREENWOOD RIDGE VINEYARDS** '89, Anderson Vly., White Riesling $8.50
			S				B		**JEKEL VINEYARDS** '90, Monterey $7.00
	B					B			**LOCKWOOD VINEYARD** '91, Monterey, Dry $8.00
					G			B	**NAVARRO VINEYARDS** '91, Mendocino $9.00
		B					B		**OBESTER WINERY** '90, Monterey Co., Ventana Vnyd. $8.00
			B					B	**PARDUCCI WINE CELLARS** '91, Central Coast $6.00
							B	S	**RANCHO SISQUOC** '91, Santa Maria Vly., Estate
		S					B		**SANTA BARBARA WINERY** '90, Santa Ynez Vly. $7.50
B		B							**TREFETHEN VINEYARDS** '90, Trefethen Vnyd., Estate $9.25
G		B							**VENTANA VINEYARDS** '90, Monterey, Ventana Vnyd. $7.00
B			S						**WILDHURST VINEYARDS** '91, Clear Lake

Johannisberg Riesling
3.1 + Residual Sugar

	L.A.	Orange	Farmers	San Fran	Dallas	State Fair	Nat'l O.S.	W. Coast	San Diego
5 AWARDS									
MOUNT PALOMAR WINERY '91, Temecula, R.S. 3.1 $6.00		S				B	S	S	G
NAVARRO VINEYARDS '90, Mendocino, LH, R.S. 7.2 $12.00	B	B	G			G	B		
3 AWARDS									
AUSTIN CELLARS '90, Santa Barbara Co., R.S. 10.0 $7.50			B				G		G
BARON HERZOG WINE CELLARS '91, Monterey Co., LH, $15.00	S			B		S			
KENDALL-JACKSON WINERY '91, California, Vintner's Reserve, R.S. 3.5 $9.00	B			B					B
KENDALL-JACKSON WINERY '90, Lake Co., Vintner's Reserve, R.S. 3.5 $9.00		B			B		G		
NAVARRO VINEYARDS '90, Mendocino, CSLH, R.S. 17.1 $25.00	G		S				G		
2 AWARDS									
BARON HERZOG WINE CELLARS '90, Monterey Co., LH, $15.00		S					G		
GEYSER PEAK WINERY '91, Russian River Vly., SSLH, R.S. 21.3 $16.00	B			B					
GEYSER PEAK WINERY '90, Mendocino Co., LH, R.S. 17.2 $13.00					G		S		
HOP KILN WINERY '91, Russian River, M. Griffin Vnyd., R.S. 5.4 $8.00		S	B						
LOCKWOOD VINEYARD '91, Monterey, SLH, R.S. 14.5	S					G			
RENAISSANCE VINEYARD '85, North Yuba, Estate SSLH, R.S. 13.0 $25.00						S	S		
WENTE BROS. '89, Arroyo Seco Vnyd., R.S. 9.8	S					B			
WINDSOR VINEYARDS '88, Russian River Vly., Estate, LH, R.S. 6.4 $12.00		B						S	

GREENWOOD
RIDGE
VINEYARDS

ANDERSON VALLEY
MERLOT
1989

ESTATE BOTTLED

ALCOHOL 12.5% BY VOLUME

1 9 8 9

CORBETT CANYON

Coastal Classic

MERLOT

C A L I F O R N I A

CELLARED AND BOTTLED BY CORBETT CANYON VINEYARDS,
EDNA VALLEY, SAN LUIS OBISPO, CALIFORNIA
Alcohol 13% by Volume

Merlot

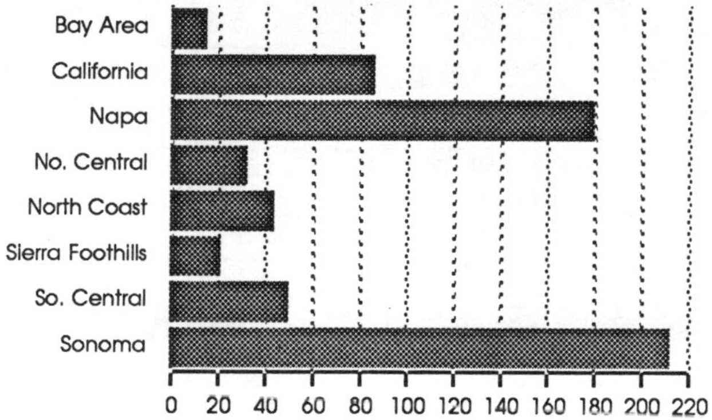

Regional Comparison of Total Points

(Gold=5 Silver=3 Bronze=1)

Highest individual wine totals

18	**GREENWOOD RIDGE VINEYARDS** '89, Anderson Vly., Estate $16.00
17	**CORBETT CANYON VINEYARDS** '89, California, Coastal Classic $8.00
16	**GUNDLACH-BUNDSCHU** '89, Sonoma Vly., Rhinefarm Vnyd., $16.00
15	**ST. CLEMENT VINEYARDS** '89, Napa Vly. $18.00
15	**BENZIGER OF GLEN ELLEN** '89, Sonoma Co. $14.00
11	**CHATEAU DE LEU WINERY** '90, Napa Vly. $12.00
11	**THOMAS JAEGER WINERY** '87, Napa Vly., Inglewood Vnyd. $15.00
11	**SHAFER VINEYARDS** '90, Napa Vly. $19.00
11	**CHATEAU JULIEN WINERY** '89, Monterey Co. $14.00
11	**CHATEAU SOUVERAIN** '90, Sonoma Co. $10.00

Merlot	L.A.	Orange	Farmers	San Fran	Dallas	State Fair	Nat'l O.S.	W. Coast	San Diego
6 AWARDS									
DRY CREEK VINEYARD '89, Dry Creek Vly. $14.00		B		S	B		B	S	B
GREENWOOD RIDGE VINEYARDS '89, Anderson Vly., Estate $16.00			S		S	S	B	S	G
GUNDLACH-BUNDSCHU '89, Sonoma Vly., Rhinefarm Vnyd., Estate $16.00	S	B				S	G	B	S
5 AWARDS									
BENZIGER OF GLEN ELLEN '89, Sonoma Co. $14.00	G	G	S				B		B
CHATEAU SOUVERAIN '89, Alexander Vly. $10.00				G	B		B	B	B
CORBETT CANYON VINEYARDS '89, California, Coastal Classic $8.00		G	G		B			G	B
GOLDEN CREEK VINEYARD '89, Sonoma Co. $12.00		S	B			S	B	B	
ST. CLEMENT VINEYARDS '89, Napa Vly. $18.00	G		B		S		S		S
4 AWARDS									
CLOS DU BOIS '89, Sonoma Co. $15.00		S			S		B	B	
CRESTON VINEYARDS '89, Paso Robles $15.00		B				B	B		G
GEYSER PEAK WINERY '89, Alexander Vly. $10.00		S			S		B	B	
GLEN ELLEN WINERY '90, California, Proprietor's Reserve $6.00		B			G		S		B
INGLENOOK-NAPA VALLEY '88, Napa Vly., Reserve $12.00		B	S	S					S
SMITH & HOOK WINERY '88, Santa Lucia Highlands, Estate $14.00	B			B		S		B	
M. G. VALLEJO WINERY '90, California $5.99		S	B				B		S
WILD HORSE WINERY '90, Central Coast $14.00	B		G			S			B
WINDSOR VINEYARDS '89, Sonoma Co. $12.00	B		S			S			B

San Diego	W. Coast	Nat'l O.S.	State Fair	Dallas	San Fran	Farmers	Orange	L.A.	Merlot
									3 AWARDS
						S	B	B	**CHAPPELLET VINEYARD** '89, Napa Vly. $16.00
G			G					B	**CHATEAU DE LEU WINERY** '90, Napa Vly. $12.00
G							B	G	**CHATEAU JULIEN WINERY** '89, Monterey Co. $14.00
			S		G			S	**CHATEAU SOUVERAIN** '90, Sonoma Co. $10.00
			B				B	B	**CLOS DU VAL** '89, Napa, Stags Leap, Estate $20.00
					B		S	B	**CONN CREEK WINERY** '89, Napa Vly. $16.00
		B	B	B					**COSENTINO WINERY** '89, Napa Vly. $18.00
		S	S					B	**FRANCISCAN OAKVILLE ESTATE** '89, Napa Vly. $15.00
B	B				B				**GARLAND RANCH** '86, California $5.00
G					B		G		**THOMAS JAEGER WINERY** '87, Napa Vly., Inglewood Vnyd. $15.00
						S	B	B	**KENDALL-JACKSON WINERY** '89, California, Vintner's Reserve $14.00
			B			S	S		**NEVADA CITY WINERY** '89, Nevada Co., Sierra Foothill $13.00
B		B					S		**NEWTON VINEYARD** '89, Napa Vly. $20.00
		B	S					S	**RAVENSWOOD** '89, Sonoma Co. $15.00
S					B		B		**RICHARDSON VINEYARDS** '90, Sonoma Vly.,Carneros, Gregory $15.00
			B				B	B	**AUGUST SEBASTIANI** 'NV, California, Country $5.00
G			B		G				**SHAFER VINEYARDS** '90, Napa Vly. $19.00
					B		G	B	**STEVENOT WINERY** '90, North Coast, Reserve $10.00
	B						S	B	**STONE CREEK CELLARS** '90, California, Special Selection $7.00

Merlot

Merlot	L.A.	Orange	Farmers	San Fran	Dallas	State Fair	Nat'l O.S.	W. Coast	San Diego
3 AWARDS									
STONY RIDGE WINERY '90, North Coast, Ltd. Release $9.00		G	B					S	
STORRS WINERY '90, Santa Clara, San Ysidro Vnyd. $13.00		B		B		G			
SWANSON VINEYARDS '90, Napa Vly. $15.00	G			S			B		
TAFT STREET WINERY '89, Sonoma Co. $11.00			B		B		B		
TRENTADUE '90, Alexander Vly., Lot 1, Estate $10.00		S				S		S	
VICHON WINERY '89, Napa Vly., Tenth Harvest $17.00	B			B					S
2 AWARDS									
BEL ARBORS 'NV, American Grown, Cask 89							G		S
BEL ARBORS '90, California $5.00	B	S							
BENZIGER OF GLEN ELLEN '89, Sonoma Mtn., Estate Bottled $20.00		S	G						
BOEGER WINERY '89, El Dorado, Estate							B		B
BOGLE VINEYARDS '90, California $6.00	B						B		
BUTTERFLY CREEK WINERY '89, Sierra Foothills, Chaple Vnyd. $15.00							B		S
DAVIS BYNUM WINERY '90, Sonoma Co., Ltd. Release $12.50	B			S					
DAVIS BYNUM WINERY '89, Sonoma Co., Ltd. Release $12.50			B				B		
CLAIRVAUX '89, Napa Vly. $12.00			S				S		
CLOS PEGASE WINERY '88, Napa Vly. $15.00				S					G
DEER VALLEY VINEYARDS '90, California		S						B	
DOMAINE NAPA WINERY '90, Napa Vly. $12.50						S			B

San Diego	W. Coast	Nat'l O.S.	State Fair	Dallas	San Fran	Farmers	Orange	L.A.	Merlot
									2 AWARDS
				S				S	**DOMAINE ST. GEORGE WINERY** '89, Sonoma Co. $8.00
		S					B		**GARY FARRELL WINES** '89, Sonoma Co., Ladi's Vnyd. $18.00
G						B			**FENESTRA WINERY** '89, Livermore Vly. $13.00
							B	S	**FIRESTONE VINEYARD** '90, Santa Ynez Vly. $12.00
		B		B					**FIRESTONE VINEYARD** '89, Santa Ynez Vly. $12.00
							S	G	**FLOREAL** '90, Napa Vly.
					S			G	**FRATELLI PERATA** '90, Paso Robles, Estate $13.00
			B		S				**GEYSER PEAK WINERY** '90, Alexander Vly. $10.00
		G				S			**GOLDEN CREEK VINEYARD** '89, Sonoma Co., Reserve $15.00
			B				G		**GUSTAVE NIEBAUM COLLECTION** '89, Napa Vly., Reference
						G		S	**INDIAN SPRINGS VINEYARDS** '89, Sierra Foothills $10.50
B	S								**KONOCTI WINERY** '89, Lake Co. $10.00
		S						B	**LAMBERT BRIDGE** '89, Dry Creek Vly. $14.00
							G	B	**LOCKWOOD VINEYARD** '90, Monterey, Estate
					S			S	**LONGORIA FAMILY WINES** '90, Santa Ynez Vly. $16.00
S				S					**PAUL MASSON VINEYARDS** '88, Monterey Co. $8.00
		B						B	**NAPA CREEK** '89, Napa Vly.
							S	B	**PARDUCCI WINE CELLARS** '90, North Coast $8.00
B							S		**RANCHO SISQUOC** '89, Santa Maria Vly.

Merlot

	L.A.	Orange	Farmers	San Fran	Dallas	State Fair	Nat'l O.S.	W. Coast	San Diego
2 AWARDS									
RETZLAFF VINEYARDS '90, Livermore Vly., Estate		B					B		
ROUND HILL CELLARS '89, Napa Vly., Reserve $11.00		B						B	
SEBASTIANI VINEYARDS '89, Sonoma Co., Family Selection		B						B	
SHAFER VINEYARDS '89, Napa Vly. $19.00					B		G		
ROBERT SINSKEY VINEYARDS '89, Napa Vly., Los Carneros $18.00	B	S							
ST. FRANCIS WINERY '89, Sonoma Vly., Estate $17.00		B				B			
VINA VISTA WINERY '88, Alexander Vly. $11.00								B	B
J. WILE & SONS '89, Napa Vly. $10.00		B					B		

VINTNER'S SELECT

1 9 9 0

DAVID BRUCE

California

Petite Syrah

PRODUCED AND BOTTLED BY DAVID BRUCE WINERY, LOS GATOS, CA
ALCOHOL 12.5% BY VOLUME CONTAINS SULFITES

Guenoc

1989
North Coast
Petite Sirah

PRODUCED AND BOTTLED BY GUENOC WINERY
MIDDLETOWN, CALIFORNIA, ALCOHOL 12.5% BY VOLUME

Petite Sirah

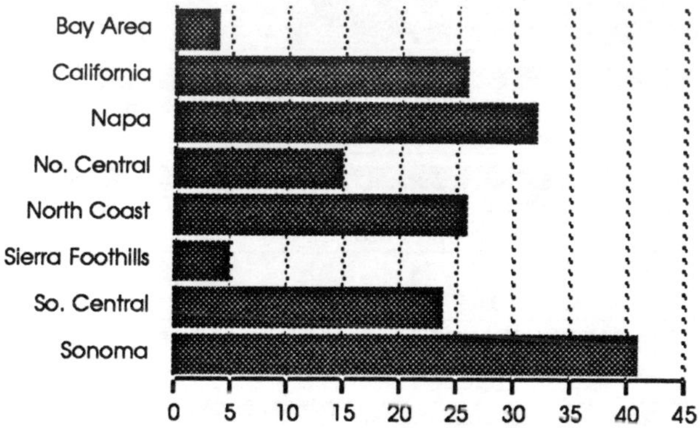

Regional Comparison of Total Points

(Gold=5 Silver=3 Bronze=1)

Highest individual wine totals

22	**DAVID BRUCE WINERY** '90, California, Vintner's Select $10.00
17	**GUENOC WINERY** '89, North Coast $14.00
14	**FOPPIANO VINEYARDS** '90, Sonoma Co. $10.00
12	**LOUIS M. MARTINI WINERY** '87, Napa Vly., Reserve $14.00
12	**IMAGERY SERIES** '88, Arroyo Seco $16.00
9	**CILURZO VINEYARD** '91, Temecula, Estate, Nouveau $7.00
8	**ROSENBLUM CELLARS** '89, Napa Vly. $12.00
7	**GEYSER PEAK WINERY** '89, Alexander Vly. $15.00
6	**GUENOC WINERY** '88, Guenoc Vly. $14.00
6	**CILURZO VINEYARD** '87, Temecula, Estate $12.00
6	**CHRISTOPHER CREEK** '88, Russian River Vly. $11.00
6	**WINDSOR VINEYARDS** '87, Sonoma Co. $10.00

Petite Sirah

	L.A.	Orange	Farmers	San Fran	Dallas	State Fair	Nat'l O.S.	W. Coast	San Diego
7 AWARDS									
GUENOC WINERY '89, North Coast $14.00	S	B	G	S	B			B	S
6 AWARDS									
DAVID BRUCE WINERY '90, California, Vintner's Select $10.00		G	B	S		G		G	S
GUENOC WINERY '88, Guenoc Vly. $14.00			B	B	B	B	B		B
LOUIS M. MARTINI WINERY '87, Napa Vly., Reserve $14.00	S	S	B	B	B				S
4 AWARDS									
CHRISTOPHER CREEK '88, Russian River Vly. $11.00	B				S		B		B
CONCANNON VINEYARD '85, Livermore Vly., Estate, Reserve $14.50			B			B		B	B
FOPPIANO VINEYARDS '90, Sonoma Co. $10.00	S			S			G	S	
IMAGERY SERIES '88, Arroyo Seco $16.00			B	G	S		S		
WINDSOR VINEYARDS '87, Sonoma Co. $10.00			B				S	B	B
3 AWARDS									
BLACK MOUNTAIN VINEYARD '88, Alexander Vly., Bosun Crest $9.00		B			B				B
CILURZO VINEYARD '91, Temecula, Estate, Nouveau $7.00		G					S		B
DEER PARK WINERY '88, Napa Vly., Howell Mt. Park/Muscatine $14.00			B	B					B
GEYSER PEAK WINERY '89, Alexander Vly. $15.00			G		B		B		
MIRASSOU VINEYARDS '89, Monterey Co., Family Selection $7.50					B		B	B	
2 AWARDS									
ARCIERO WINERY '87, Paso Robles, Estate $7.00		S		B					
BOGLE VINEYARDS '90, California $6.00		B	S						

Petite Sirah

2 AWARDS

San Diego	W. Coast	Nat'l O.S.	State Fair	Dallas	San Fran	Farme's	Orange	L.A.	Petite Sirah
			G		B				**CILURZO VINEYARD** '87, Temecula, Estate $12.00
		G		S					**ROSENBLUM CELLARS** '89, Napa Vly. $12.00

STONESTREET
1990
PINOT NOIR
Russian River Valley

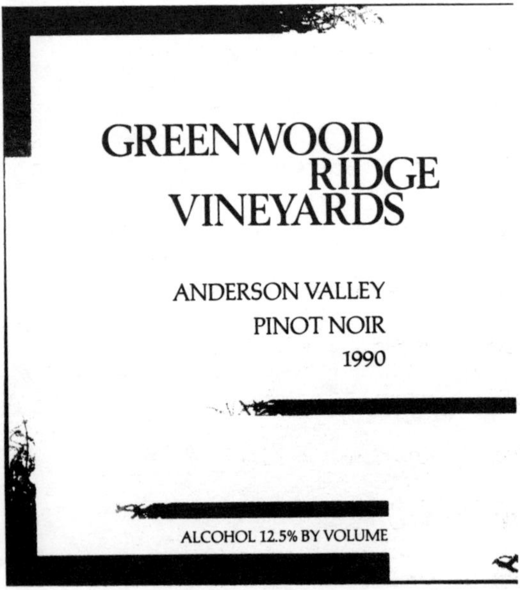
GREENWOOD
RIDGE
VINEYARDS
ANDERSON VALLEY
PINOT NOIR
1990
ALCOHOL 12.5% BY VOLUME

Pinot Noir

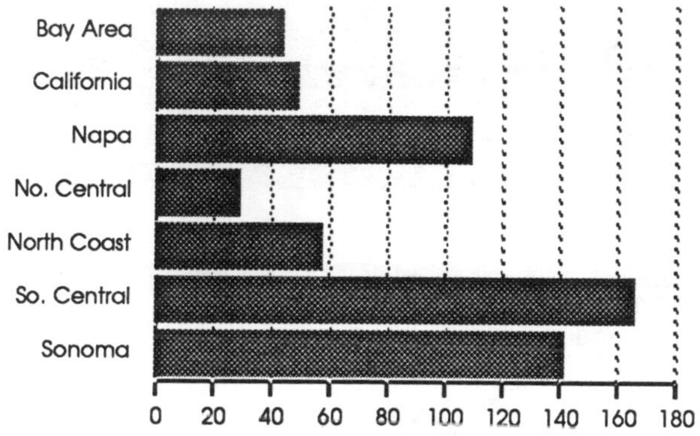

Regional Comparison of Total Points

(Gold=5 Silver=3 Bronze=1)

Highest individual wine totals

25	**J. STONESTREET & SONS** '90, Russian River Vly. $30.00
19	**GREENWOOD RIDGE VINEYARDS** '90, Anderson Vly. $15.00
17	**GARY FARRELL WINES** '90, Russian River Vly., Allen Vnyd. $28.00
15	**DAVID BRUCE WINERY** '89, Santa Cruz Mtns., Estate $22.00
15	**CAMBRIA WINERY** '89, Santa Maria Vly., Julia's Vnyd. $16.00
15	**CHEVAL SAUVAGE** '90, Santa Barbara Co. $25.00
15	**RODNEY STRONG VINEYARDS** '90, Russian River Vly., River East Vnyd. $12.00
14	**WESTWOOD WINERY** '90, California
14	**CRESTON VINEYARDS** '90, Paso Robles $9.00
13	**CHEVAL SAUVAGE** '90, Paso Robles $25.00
12	**DAVID BRUCE WINERY** '89, S. Barbara/Sonoma/SLO, Vint. Sel. $12.00
12	**GARY FARRELL WINES** '90, Russian River Vly. $16.00

Pinot Noir

7 AWARDS

Winery / Wine	L.A.	Orange	Farmers	San Fran	Dallas	State Fair	Nat'l O.S.	W. Coast	San Diego
GARY FARRELL WINES '90, Russian River Vly., Allen Vnyd. $28.00		G	G	B	B	B		B	S

6 AWARDS

Winery / Wine	L.A.	Orange	Farmers	San Fran	Dallas	State Fair	Nat'l O.S.	W. Coast	San Diego
CRESTON VINEYARDS '90, Paso Robles $9.00	B	G	B			B	G	B	

5 AWARDS

Winery / Wine	L.A.	Orange	Farmers	San Fran	Dallas	State Fair	Nat'l O.S.	W. Coast	San Diego
DAVID BRUCE WINERY '89, Santa Cruz Mtns., Estate $22.00		B	G	G		B			S
CAMBRIA WINERY '89, Santa Maria Vly., Julia's Vnyd. $16.00		G	S	B	B	G			
CHATEAU DE LEU WINERY '90, Napa Vly. $12.00		S		B		S		B	B
CHEVAL SAUVAGE '90, Santa Barbara Co. $25.00	S	S		B		G		S	
DEHLINGER WINERY '89, Russian River Vly., Estate $16.50		B	S		S	B		B	
GREENWOOD RIDGE VINEYARDS '90, Anderson Vly. $15.00		B	G		S	G			G
J. STONESTREET & SONS '90, Russian River Vly. $30.00			G	G		G		G	G
RODNEY STRONG VINEYARDS '90, Russian River Vly., River East Vnyd. $12.00	B	G				S		G	B

4 AWARDS

Winery / Wine	L.A.	Orange	Farmers	San Fran	Dallas	State Fair	Nat'l O.S.	W. Coast	San Diego
BON MARCHE '91, Sonoma Co. $8.00	B	B	B					G	
DAVID BRUCE WINERY '89, S. Barbara/Sonoma/SLO, Vint. Sel. $12.00		B		G	G	B			
GARY FARRELL WINES '90, Russian River Vly. $16.00		B	G			S			S
TOBIN JAMES '90, Santa Barbara Co., Sunshine $15.00	B	B		B					S
KENDALL-JACKSON WINERY '89, California, Vintner's Reserve $13.00			B	B	S	B			
ROCHIOLI VINEYARD '90, Russian River Vly., Estate $16.00		B				B		S	S

Pinot Noir

San Diego	W. Coast	Nat'l O.S.	State Fair	Dallas	San Fran	Farmers	Orange	L.A.	Pinot Noir
									4 AWARDS
S			S				S	G	**WESTWOOD WINERY** '90, California
B			S		B		B		**YORK MOUNTAIN WINERY** '87, San Luis Obispo, Reserve $16.00
									3 AWARDS
G					S		S		**DAVID BRUCE WINERY** '89, Santa Cruz Mtn., Estate, Reserve $27.00
			S	B			B		**CARNEROS CREEK WINERY** '89, Los Carneros $14.50
			S				G	G	**CHEVAL SAUVAGE** '90, Paso Robles $25.00
		B			S		S		**GARY FARRELL WINES** '90, Santa Barbara Co., Bien Nacido Vnyd. $24.00
				B	G	B			**THOMAS FOGARTY WINERY** '89, Santa Cruz Mtn., Estate $16.00
	S		B				G		**KENWOOD VINEYARDS** '90, Sonoma Vly., Jack London Vnyd. $15.00
	B	S					B		**MIRASSOU VINEYARDS** '90, Monterey Co.,5th Gen. Family Sel. $7.50
B					B		S		**ROBERT MONDAVI WINERY** '90, Napa Vly. $14.00
		B				G	S		**MONTEREY VINEYARD** '89, Monterey Co., Ltd. Release $8.00
		S			B			S	**KENT RASMUSSEN WINERY** '90, Carneros $18.00
B		S		S					**SANFORD WINERY** '89, Santa Barbara Co. $16.00
						G	G	B	**SEGHESIO WINERY** '89, Sonoma Co. $9.00
									2 AWARDS
			B			B			**APTOS VINEYARD** '89, Santa Cruz Co. $11.95
						B		S	**BOUCHAINE VINEYARDS** '89, Napa Vly, Carneros $15.00

Pinot Noir

	L.A.	Orange	Farmers	San Fran	Dallas	State Fair	Nat'l O.S.	W. Coast	San Diego
2 AWARDS									
BRANDBORG CELLARS '90, Bien Nacido Vnyd. $13.00	G			B					
BUENA VISTA WINERY '89, Carneros, Estate $9.00			B						B
BYRON VINEYARD '90, Santa Barbara Co. $13.00					S				B
BYRON VINEYARD '89, Santa Barbara Co., Reserve $20.00			S					B	
CHATEAU DE BAUN WINERY '90, California, Barrel Sel., Chateau Rouge $6.00		B				B			
CLOS DU VAL '88, Napa Vly., Carneros $14.00	B			B					
CORBETT CANYON VINEYARDS '90, Santa Barbara Co., Reserve $9.00	S	S							
DOMAINE DE CLARCK '90, Monterey Co., Villages		B				S			
FIDDLEHEAD CELLARS '90, Santa Maria Vly. $25.00		B	G						
GUNDLACH-BUNDSCHU '90, Sonoma Co., Rhinefarm Vnyd. $14.00	B					S			
HUSCH VINEYARDS '89, Anderson Vly., Estate $14.00		S	B						
LA CREMA '89, California $12.00					B	G			
LEEWARD WINERY '90, Santa Barbara Co. $16.00	B					S			
LOUIS M. MARTINI WINERY '88, Napa Vly., Carneros, La Loma Vnyd. $13.99	S		B						
MC HENRY VINEYARD '88, Santa Cruz Mtns. $12.50	B					S			
MERIDIAN VINEYARDS '90, Santa Barbara Co. $14.00		S	B						
ROBERT MONDAVI WINERY '90, Napa Vly., Unfiltered, Reserve $28.00					B				G
MORGAN '90, California $14.00		S			G				

San Diego	W. Coast	Nat'l O.S.	State Fair	Dallas	San Fran	Farmers	Orange	L.A.	Pinot Noir
									2 AWARDS
		G					B		**NAPA RIDGE** '90, North Coast $6.00
		G			S				**NAVARRO VINEYARDS** '89, Anderson Vly., Methode L'Ancienne $14.00
						B	G		**NAVARRO VINEYARDS** '89, Mendocino, Table Wine $8.00
						S	G		**NAVARRO VINEYARDS** '88, Anderson Vly., Methode A L'Ancienne $14.00
					B			G	**NEWLAN VINEYARDS** '89, Napa Vly. $18.00
							B	B	**PARDUCCI WINE CELLARS** '90, Mendocino Co. $6.00
						B		S	**ROCHIOLI VINEYARD** '90, Sonoma Co. $16.00
	B						B		**ROSENBLUM CELLARS** '90, Napa Vly., George Hendry Vnyd. $13.00
			B		B				**SANFORD WINERY** '90, Santa Barbara Co. $16.00
		B	S						**SANTA CRUZ MOUNTAIN** '88, Santa Cruz Mtns., Estate
			B			S			**SCHUG CELLARS** '88, Carneros, Beckstoffer Vnyd. $13.00
			S				B		**ROBERT SINSKEY VINEYARDS** '90, Napa Vly., Los Carneros $18.00
G						S			**STERLING VINEYARDS** '89, Carneros, Winery Lake $14.00
							S	G	**WESTWOOD WINERY** '89, Napa Vly., Haynes Vnyd., Reserve
			S		B				**WILD HORSE WINERY** '90, Santa Barbara Co. $12.00
B				S					**ZACA MESA WINERY** '89, Santa Barbara Co., Reserve $16.00
	G		B						**ZD WINES** '90, Napa Vly., Carneros $17.00

LANGTRY

1989
BENZIGER
SONOMA MOUNTAIN
A TRIBUTE

Red Meritage

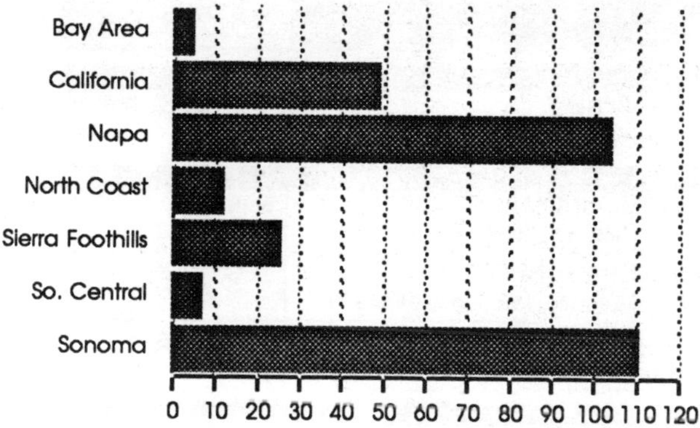

Regional Comparison of Total Points

(Gold=5 Silver=3 Bronze=1)

Highest individual wine totals

20 **GUENOC WINERY**
'88, Napa Co./Lake Co., Langtry $35.00

19 **MOUNT VEEDER WINERY**
'88, Napa Vly., Red Table Wine $24.00

19 **BENZIGER OF GLEN ELLEN**
'89, Sonoma Mtn., A Tribute $25.00

17 **GOLD HILL VINEYARD**
'89, El Dorado, Estate $16.00

15 **CONN CREEK WINERY**
'87, Napa Vly., Triomphe $26.00

15 **GEYSER PEAK WINERY**
'87, Alexander Vly., Res. Alexandre $20.00

14 **TOPAZ WINES**
'88, Napa Vly., Rouge De Trois $15.00

14 **DE LORIMIER WINERY**
'87, Alexander Vly., Mosaic $18.00

13 **DRY CREEK VINEYARD**
'87, Dry Creek Vly. $24.00

12 **GOLDEN CREEK VINEYARD**
'89, Sonoma Co., Caberlot $12.00

11 **RICHARDSON VINEYARDS**
'89, Sonoma/Napa Vly., Synergy $15.00

Red Meritage

Wine	L.A.	Orange	Farmers	San Fran	Dallas	State Fair	Nat'l O.S.	W. Coast	San Diego
8 AWARDS									
GUENOC WINERY '88, Napa Co./Lake Co., Langtry $35.00		G	B	G	B	B	S	S	B
7 AWARDS									
DRY CREEK VINEYARD '87, Dry Creek Vly. $24.00	B	B	B			B	G	B	S
GEYSER PEAK WINERY '87, Alexander Vly., Res. Alexandre $20.00		G		B	B	S	B	S	B
MOUNT VEEDER WINERY '88, Napa Vly., Red Table Wine $24.00	B	S	G	B	S			B	G
6 AWARDS									
DE LORIMIER WINERY '87, Alexander Vly., Mosaic $18.00	G	G		B	B	B			B
FRANCISCAN OAKVILLE ESTATE '88, Napa Vly., Red Table Wine $20.00	B	B	B		B		B		G
5 AWARDS									
BENZIGER OF GLEN ELLEN '89, Sonoma Mtn., A Tribute $25.00	B	S	G	G					G
CONN CREEK WINERY '87, Napa Vly., Triomphe $26.00	G	G		B				S	B
GOLD HILL VINEYARD '89, El Dorado, Estate $16.00	S	S		B		G		G	
NEVADA CITY WINERY '89, Sierra Foothills, Dir. Reserve $14.00		B		B		B		G	B
RICHARDSON VINEYARDS '89, Sonoma/Napa Vly., Synergy $15.00		B	S	B		G		B	
STERLING VINEYARDS '88, Napa Vly., Sterling Reserve $40.00			S	B	S		B		B
4 AWARDS									
CLOS DU BOIS '88, Alexander Vly., Marlstone $20.00		B			S		S	S	
GOLDEN CREEK VINEYARD '89, Sonoma Co., Caberlot $12.00			S		S		G	B	
TOPAZ WINES '88, Napa Vly., Rouge De Trois $15.00		G		B			G	S	
3 AWARDS									
BRANDER VINEYARD '89, Bouchet Tete De Cuvee $20.00			B				B		S

Red Meritage

San Diego	W. Coast	Nat'l O.S.	State Fair	Dallas	San Fran	Farmers	Orange	L.A.	Wine
									3 AWARDS
			G		B			B	**CLOS DU BOIS** '89, Alexander Vly., Marlstone $20.00
	S	B				S			**HACIENDA WINERY** '88, Sonoma Co., Antares $28.00
	G	B						B	**KONRAD ESTATE** '89, Mendocino, Melange A Trois
	S					B	S		**ANTHONY D. MATERA WINE CELLARS** 'NV, Napa Vly., Medley $10.72
									2 AWARDS
					B		S		**COS** '89, Napa Vly. $45.00
S		S							**ESTANCIA VINEYARDS** '89, Alexander Vly. $14.00
					B		B		**FLORA SPRINGS** '88, Napa Vly., Trilogy $33.00
					B		S		**GUENOC WINERY** '89, Lake Co. $35.00
			G				S		**KENDALL-JACKSON WINERY** '87, Cardinale $65.00
B							G		**NEWTON VINEYARD** '90, Napa Vly., Claret, Meritage
							B	B	**RAVENSWOOD** '89, Sonoma Mtn., Pickberry Vnyd. $26.00
B						B			**STERLING VINEYARDS** '88, Napa Vly., Three Palms Vnyd. $23.00

GEYSER PEAK
TRIONE CELLARS
CALIFORNIA
SONOMA COUNTY
SAUVIGNON BLANC

Since 1857
Buena Vista
Lake County
SAUVIGNON
BLANC
ALC. 12.5% BY VOL.

Sauvignon Blanc

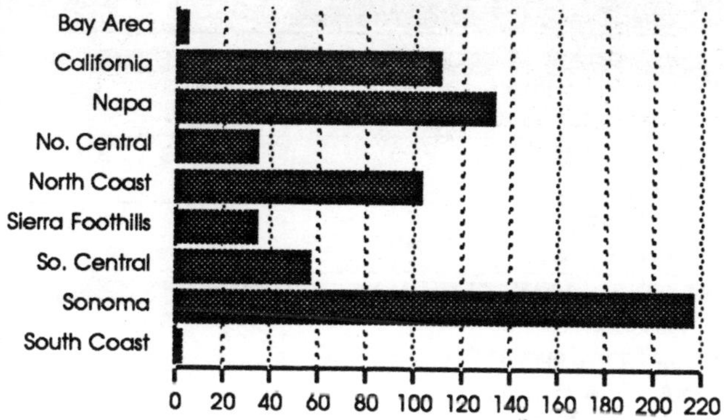

Regional Comparison of Total Points

(Gold=5 Silver=3 Bronze=1)

Highest individual wine totals

16 **BEL ARBORS**
'90, California, Founders Selection $5.00

15 **GEYSER PEAK WINERY**
'90, Sonoma Co. $6.50

14 **LAKESPRING WINERY**
'91, Napa Vly., Yount Mill Vnyd. $8.50

14 **BUENA VISTA WINERY**
'91, Lake Co. $7.00

14 **GEYSER PEAK WINERY**
'91, Sonoma Co $7.00

14 **ROCHIOLI VINEYARD**
'91, Russian River Vly., Estate $9.00

13 **MONTEVINA WINES**
'91, California, Fume $6.50

12 **LOUIS M. MARTINI WINERY**
'90, Napa Vly. $7.00

10 **CLOS PEGASE WINERY**
'89, Napa Vly. $9.50

10 **HANDLEY CELLARS**
'90, Dry Creek Vly. $8.00

Sauvignon Blanc

	L.A.	Orange	Farmers	San Fran	Dallas	State Fair	Nat'l O.S.	W. Coast	San Diego
5 AWARDS									
GEYSER PEAK WINERY '90, Sonoma Co. $6.50			B	S			G	S	S
KONOCTI WINERY '90, Lake Co. Fume $7.50			B	B		B		S	B
QUAIL RIDGE CELLARS '90, Napa Vly. $8.00		B	S	B		B	B		
4 AWARDS									
BEL ARBORS '90, California, Founders Selection $5.00		G		S			G		S
BUENA VISTA WINERY '91, Lake Co. $7.00	S	S		G		S			
DAVIS BYNUM WINERY '91, Russian River Vly. Fume $8.00		B	B	S					B
CLOS PEGASE WINERY '89, Napa Vly. $9.50			S				G	B	B
GEYSER PEAK WINERY '91, Sonoma Co $7.00	S	G		G		B			
HANDLEY CELLARS '90, Dry Creek Vly. $8.00			S		B			S	S
KENDALL-JACKSON WINERY '90, Califonia, Vintner's Reserve $9.00	B		B		B			S	
LAKESPRING WINERY '91, Napa Vly., Yount Mill Vnyd. $8.50	G	G				S		B	
LOUIS M. MARTINI WINERY '90, Napa Vly. $7.00		G	B	S				S	
QUIVIRA VINEYARDS '90, Dry Creek Vly. $10.00				B	B		S		B
RAYMOND VINEYARD '90, Napa Vly. $9.75		B	B	B					S
ROCHIOLI VINEYARD '91, Russian River Vly., Estate $9.00	G	S				B		G	
VENTANA VINEYARDS '90, Monterey, Estate $8.00		S	B				S		B
3 AWARDS									
ADLER FELS WINERY '90, Sonoma Co., Fume $9.00					S	B	G		
ALDERBROOK WINERY '90, Dry Creek Vly., Estate $8.00				B				B	B

Sauvignon Blanc

3 AWARDS

San Diego	W. Coast	Nat'l O.S.	State Fair	Dallas	San Fran	Farmers	Orange	L.A.	Winery
B		S				B			**BAREFOOT CELLARS** 'NV, California $5.00
S						S	B		**BEAULIEU VINEYARD** '89, Napa Vly., Beautour Fume $7.75
				S		B	B		**BENZIGER OF GLEN ELLEN** '90, Sonoma Co. Fume $9.00
	S				B		S		**CHATEAU DE LEU WINERY** '90, Napa Vly. $6.00
B						S	G		**CHATEAU POTELLE** '91, Napa Vly. $8.95
	S	S		S					**CORBETT CANYON VINEYARDS** '91, Central Coast, Coastal Classic $6.00
			B		S		B		**DE LOACH VINEYARDS** '91, Russian River Vly. $10.00
		B		S		S			**DE LOACH VINEYARDS** '90, Russian River Vly., Fume $9.50
B	B			S					**DOMAINE BRETON** '90, North Coast $7.00
	S	B					S		**DOMAINE NAPA WINERY** '90, Napa Co. $10.00
	B				S		S		**E. & J. GALLO** '89, California, Reserve $5.00
		B			B		S		**GLEN ELLEN WINERY** '91, California, Prop. Reserve $5.00
		B			S	S			**HAYWOOD WINERY** '90, Sonoma Vly., Los Chamizal $10.00
					S	B	S		**LAVA CAP WINERY** '90, El Dorado, Estate, Fume $7.00
			B		B			G	**MARKHAM VINEYARDS** '91, Napa Vly. $8.00
	G		S				G		**MONTEVINA WINES** '91, California, Fume $6.50
	S				S		B		**MOUNT PALOMAR WINERY** '91, Temecula $8.00
		B				B		S	**PARDUCCI WINE CELLARS** '90, North Coast $6.00
			S		B		B		**RENAISSANCE VINEYARD** '84, North Yuba, Estate, LH $14.00

Sauvignon Blanc

	L.A.	Orange	Farmers	San Fran	Dallas	State Fair	Nat'l O.S.	W. Coast	San Diego
3 AWARDS									
SIMI WINERY '90, Sonoma/Mendocino/Napa $8.75					B		S		B
ST. CLEMENT VINEYARDS '91, Napa Vly. $10.00		S						B	B
RODNEY STRONG VINEYARDS '90, Sonoma, Charlottes Home Vnyd. $9.00			B		B				B
WINDSOR VINEYARDS '91, Alexander Vly., Fume $10.00	B							S	B
2 AWARDS									
AUDUBON CELLARS '89, Napa Vly.	B						S		
BANDIERA WINERY '90, Napa Co. $5.00		S		B					
BARON HERZOG WINE CELLARS '91, California $9.00				G		S			
BENZIGER OF GLEN ELLEN '90, Sonoma Mtn., Estate $14.00		B	G						
BRANDER VINEYARD '90, Santa Ynez, Tete De Cuvee $9.75		B	B						
BUENA VISTA WINERY '90, Lake Co. $7.00					B		S		
BYRON VINEYARD '91, Santa Barbara Co. $9.00	B			B					
BYRON VINEYARD '90, Santa Barbara Co. $9.00					B				S
CALLAWAY VINEYARD '90, Temecula $8.00	S	B							
CLOS DU BOIS '91, Alexander Vly., Barrel Ferm. $8.00		S						B	
DE MOOR WINERY '90, Napa Vly.		B					B		
DELICATO VINEYARDS '89, Monterey $5.00		B					S		
DOMAINE ST. GEORGE WINERY '90, Alexander Vly., Fume, Reserve		B							S
DRY CREEK VINEYARD '90, Sonoma Co., Fume $9.25					B		B		

Sauvignon Blanc

2 AWARDS

San Diego	W. Coast	Nat'l O.S.	State Fair	Dallas	San Fran	Farmers	Orange	L.A.	Wine
			B				S		**ESTANCIA VINEYARDS** '91, Monterey $7.50
					S			B	**FETZER VINEYARDS** '91, California, Fume $7.00
	B						B		**FETZER VINEYARDS** '90, California, Barrel Select $9.00
			G				B		**FIELDBROOK VALLEY WINERY** '91, Mendocino Co., Quillen Vnyd.
	B						B		**FIRESTONE VINEYARD** '91, Santa Ynez Vly.
					B		B		**J. FRITZ WINERY** '91, Dry Creek Vly. $8.00
		B		G					**J. FRITZ WINERY** '90, Dry Creek Vly. $8.00
			B					B	**J. FURST** '91, California
	B		S						**GAINEY VINEYARD** '90, Santa Ynez Vly. $15.00
	B			G					**GRAND CRU VINEYARDS** '90, Sonoma Co., Prem. Selection $9.50
					S		G		**HUSCH VINEYARDS** '91, Mendocino, La Ribera Vnyd. $8.50
		S		B					**HUSCH VINEYARDS** '90, Mendocino, La Ribera Vnyds. $8.50
S						B			**THOMAS JAEGER WINERY** '90, San Diego Co. $8.98
						B	B		**JOUILLIAN VINEYARD** '90, Carmel Vly. $6.00
					B			S	**KENWOOD VINEYARDS** '91, Sonoma Co. $10.00
		B					B		**LAMBERT BRIDGE** '90, Sonoma Co., Fume $10.00
S				S					**LOLONIS WINERY** '90, Mendocino Co., Fume
B							B		**MATANZAS CREEK WINERY** '90, Sonoma Co.
						B	S		**J. W. MORRIS WINERY** '89, California, Reserve $6.50

Sauvignon Blanc

2 AWARDS

Wine	L.A.	Orange	Farmers	San Fran	Dallas	State Fair	Nat'l O.S.	W. Coast	San Diego
NAVARRO VINEYARDS '90, Mendocino $9.75		B	G						
ROBERT PEPI WINERY '91, Napa Vly. $10.00				B		B			
R. H. PHILLIPS VINEYARD '91, Dunnigan Hills, Night Harvest $5.00	G				B				
R. H. PHILLIPS VINEYARD '91, California, Night Harvest $6.00				B				S	
ROUMIGUIERE VINEYARDS '90, Lake Co. Fume $7.50			B				G		
RUTHERFORD HILL WINERY '90, Napa Vly. $9.00		B	B						
ST. SUPERY WINERY '90, Napa Vly., Dollarhide Ranch $8.50							B	B	
STONE CREEK CELLARS '91, Napa Vly. Fume, Special Sel. $6.00		S							B
VENDANGE '91, California $5.00		B						S	
WHITE OAK VINEYARDS '90, Sonoma Co. $8.95					S		B		

Fifth Generation Cuvée
Mirassou
1989
Monterey Champagne
BLANC DE NOIRS
ALCOHOL 11% BY VOLUME • 750 ML

Napa Valley
BLANC DE NOIRS
California
METHODE CHAMPENOISE
NAPA VALLEY SPARKLING WINE
750 ML (25.4 FL. OZ.)
ALC. 12.0% BY VOL.

Sparkling Wine

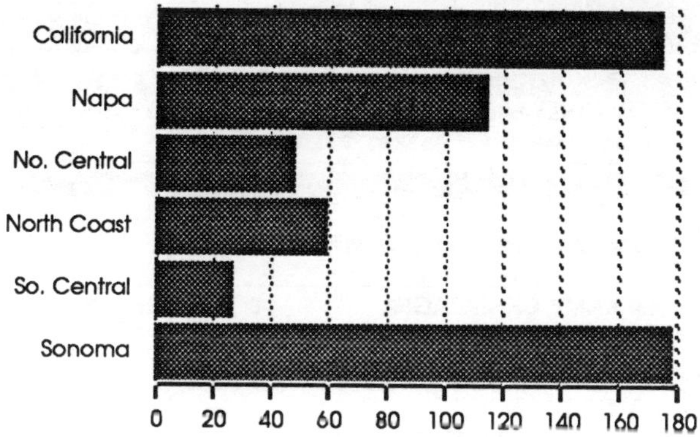

Regional Comparison of Total Points

(Gold=5 Silver=3 Bronze=1)

Highest individual wine totals

22 **BALLATORE CHAMPAGNE**
'NV, California, Gran Spumante $5.50

22 **MUMM NAPA VALLEY**
'NV, Cuvee Napa, Brut Prestige $15.00

22 **MIRASSOU VINEYARDS**
'89, 5th Gen. Cuvee Blanc De Noirs $12.00

21 **SCHARFFENBERGER**
'88, Mendocino, Blanc De Blanc $22.00

19 **VAN DER KAMP CHAMPAGNE**
'86, Sonoma Vly., English Cuvee $15.00

18 **HANDLEY CELLARS**
'87, Anderson Vly., Brut $15.00

17 **MUMM NAPA VALLEY**
'NV, Napa, Cuvee Napa Blanc De Noirs $15.00

15 **WINDSOR VINEYARDS**
'NV, California, Extra Dry, Lot 1 $8.00

14 **VAN DER KAMP CHAMPAGNE**
'88, Sonoma Vly., Midnight Cuvee $15.00

13 **GLORIA FERRER**
'NV, Sonoma Co. Brut $14.00

13 **WINDSOR VINEYARDS**
'87, Sonoma Co., Blanc De Blanc $18.00

Sparkling Wine

0 - 1.5 Residual Sugar

	L.A.	Orange	Farmers	San Fran	Dallas	State Fair	Nat'l O.S.	W. Coast	San Diego
8 AWARDS									
MIRASSOU VINEYARDS '89, 5th Gen. Cuvee Blanc De Noirs $12.00	G	G	B	B	S	G		B	B
7 AWARDS									
MUMM NAPA VALLEY 'NV, Napa, Cuvee Napa Blanc De Noirs $15.00	B	S	S	S	B		S		S
VAN DER KAMP CHAMPAGNE '86, Sonoma Vly., English Cuvee $15.00	B	S	B	S		S	G		S
6 AWARDS									
HANDLEY CELLARS '87, Anderson Vly., Brut $15.00		G		G	B	B		G	B
MAISON DEUTZ WINERY 'NV, SLO/Santa Barbara Brut Rose $24.00		B	B		B	B		G	B
MUMM NAPA VALLEY 'NV, Cuvee Napa, Brut Prestige $15.00	G	S	G			S	G		B
VAN DER KAMP CHAMPAGNE '88, Sonoma Vly., Midnight Cuvee $15.00	G		G	B	B		B		B
5 AWARDS									
BENZIGER OF GLEN ELLEN '88, Carneros, Brut, Blanc De Blancs $14.00	S	S	B	B					S
CULBERTSON WINERY 'NV, California, Brut $12.00		B			G	B		B	S
GLORIA FERRER 'NV, Sonoma Co. Brut $14.00	S	S	S					B	S
MAISON DEUTZ WINERY '87, San Luis Obispo Co.,Brut Reserve $22.00	S	S	S		B		B		
MIRASSOU VINEYARDS '88, Monterey,au Naturel, 5th Gen. Cuvee $15.00	B	S				B	G		B
SCHARFFENBERGER '88, Mendocino, Blanc De Blanc $22.00	G	G	B	G		G			
WINDSOR VINEYARDS '87, Sonoma Co., Blanc De Blanc $18.00	S	S		S			B	S	
4 AWARDS									
S. ANDERSON VINEYARD '87, Napa Vly., Blanc De Noirs $20.00	S				B		S	S	

Sparkling Wine
0 - 1.5 Residual Sugar

San Diego	W. Coast	Nat'l O.S.	State Fair	Dallas	San Fran	Farmers	Orange	L.A.	Wine
4 AWARDS									
		B	B			S		B	**MAISON DEUTZ WINERY** 'NV, SLO/Santa Barbara Co., Brut Cuvee $15.00
	B				B		G	S	**WINDSOR VINEYARDS** '87, Sonoma Co., Brut $13.00
3 AWARDS									
			B				S	B	**CHASE LIMOGERE** 'NV, California, Brut $6.00
		S		B			G		**CHATEAU DE BAUN WINERY** '88, Sonoma Co., Rhapsody, Brut Rose $11.00
		S		G			B		**CHATEAU DE BAUN WINERY** '88, Sonoma Co., Romance, Brut $11.00
			B				B	G	**CHATEAU ST. JEAN** 'NV, Sonoma Co., Blanc De Blanc $12.00
B			B				S		**CHATEAU ST. JEAN** 'NV, Sonoma Co., Brut $12.00
S		B	B						**CULBERTSON WINERY** '87, California, Natural $16.00
					B	B	B		**GLORIA FERRER** '87, Carneros, Brut $17.00
B		B		B					**FOLIE A DEUX WINERY** '89, Napa Vly., Fantasie $18.00
B	B			B					**MIRASSOU VINEYARDS** '84, Monterey, 5th Gen. Cuvee Brut, Res. $15.00
				B		S	G		**MUMM NAPA VALLEY** '88, Winery Lake, Cuvee Napa, Brut $22.00
		S		S			S		**MUMM NAPA VALLEY** '87, Cuvee Napa, Vintage Res. Brut $22.00
			B		B			B	**WINDSOR VINEYARDS** '88, Sonoma Co., Brut Rose $12.00
	B						S	B	**WINDSOR VINEYARDS** '87, Sonoma Co., Blanc De Noir $13.00
2 AWARDS									
	S			B					**S. ANDERSON VINEYARD** '86, Napa Vly., Brut $20.00
							S	S	**BYRON VINEYARD** 'NV, Santa Barbara, Brut, Res. $18.00

Sparkling Wine

0 - 1.5 Residual Sugar

Wine	L.A.	Orange	Farmers	San Fran	Dallas	State Fair	Nat'l O.S.	W. Coast	San Diego
2 AWARDS									
CULBERTSON WINERY '86, California, Blanc De Blanc $20.00			B					B	
DOMAINE CARNEROS 'NV, Carneros, Brut $17.00		G	B						
DOMAINE MONTREAUX '86, Napa Vly. Brut		B						B	
DUSINBERRE WINERY '90, Napa Vly., Marston Vnyd.	B								B
GLORIA FERRER '85, Carneros Cuvee, Brut $20.00		S			S				
THOMAS FOGARTY WINERY '89, Santa Cruz Mtns., Brut		B						B	
J '88, Sonoma Co., Brut $22.00		G		B					
MARK WEST VINEYARDS '86, Russian River Vly. Blanc De Noirs $17.00	B							S	
MIRASSOU VINEYARDS '88, Monterey, 5th Generation Cuvee, Brut		G				B			
QUINTESSENCE '88, Napa Vly., Blanc De Blanc, Brut		G	B						
SCHARFFENBERGER 'NV, Mendocino Co., Brut $18.00			S			S			
SCHARFFENBERGER 'NV, Mendocino Co., Brut Rose	S	S							

Sparkling Wine

1.6 + Residual Sugar

San Diego	W. Coast	Nat'l O.S.	State Fair	Dallas	San Fran	Farmers	Orange	L.A.	Wine
									8 AWARDS
B	G	S	G		B	S	B	S	**BALLATORE CHAMPAGNE** 'NV, California, Gran Spumante $5.50
									5 AWARDS
	B		B	B			S	S	**COOKS CHAMPAGNE CELLARS** 'NV, American, Imperial White Zinfandel $3.99
S		B		B	B		G		**CULBERTSON WINERY** 'NV, California Blanc De Noirs $12.00
B		B	B				G	B	**CULBERTSON WINERY** 'NV, California, Cuvee De Frontignan $16.00
		B	S	B			B	B	**CULBERTSON WINERY** 'NV, California, Cuvee Rouge $12.00
S	B	S					G	S	**WINDSOR VINEYARDS** 'NV, California, Extra Dry, Lot 1 $8.00
									4 AWARDS
	B		S				S	B	**COOKS CHAMPAGNE CELLARS** 'NV, American Spumante $3.99
B		B				B		S	**TOTT'S CHAMPAGNE CELLARS** 'NV, California, Extra Dry $7.50
									3 AWARDS
			S				S	B	**COOKS CHAMPAGNE CELLARS** 'NV, American, Imperial Blush $3.99
	B			B				S	**TOTT'S CHAMPAGNE CELLARS** 'NV, California, Brut, Reserve Cuvee $7.50
									2 AWARDS
			S				B		**COOKS CHAMPAGNE CELLARS** 'NV, American, Imperial Extra Dry $3.99
				S			B		**CULBERTSON WINERY** '87, California, Brut Rose
B	S								**SEBASTIANI VINEYARDS** '87, Sonoma Co., Richard Cuneo Cuvee

LANGTRY

1990
LAKEWOOD™
Meritage
86% Semillon, 14% Sauvignon Blanc
California
White Table Wine
KENDALL-JACKSON
ALCOHOL 13.5% BY VOLUME

White Meritage

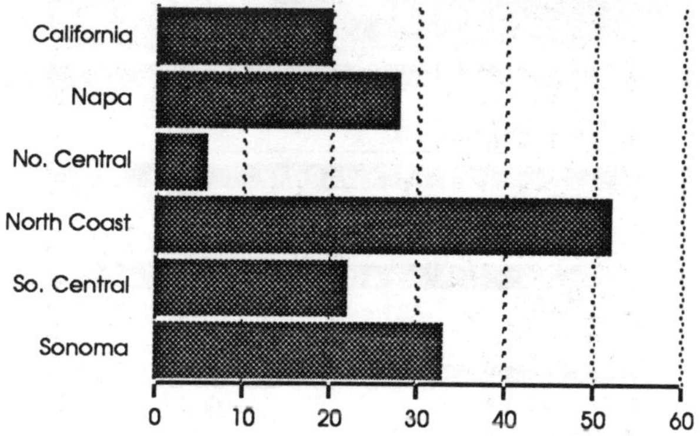

Regional Comparison of Total Points

(Gold=5 Silver=3 Bronze=1)

Highest individual wine totals

25	**GUENOC WINERY** '90, Guenoc Vly., Langtry $17.00
18	**LAKEWOOD VINEYARDS** '90, California $15.00
16	**GABRIELLI WINERY** '90, Mendocino, Ascenza $12.00
11	**BAILY VINEYARD** '91, Temecula, Montage $11.00
9	**KONOCTI WINERY** '89, Clear Lake, Estate $14.00
9	**BENZIGER OF GLEN ELLEN** '90, Sonoma Mtn., A Tribute $17.00
9	**GEYSER PEAK WINERY** '91, Alexander Vly., Chateau Alexandre $13.00
8	**TOPAZ WINES** '89, Napa Vly., SSLH $8.50
7	**DE LORIMIER WINERY** '90, Alexander Vly., Spectrum $9.00
6	**MERRYVALE VINEYARDS** '91, Napa Vly. $12.00
6	**VICHON WINERY** '90, Napa Vly., Chevrignon $9.60
6	**CRESTON VINEYARDS** '91, Paso Robles, Estate, Chevrier Blanc $9.00

White Meritage

	L.A.	Orange	Farmers	San Fran	Dallas	State Fair	Nat'l O.S.	W. Coast	San Diego
9 AWARDS									
GUENOC WINERY '90, Guenoc Vly., Langtry $17.00	G	S	G	B	B	G	B	S	B
6 AWARDS									
GABRIELLI WINERY '90, Mendocino, Ascenza $12.00		S	S	S		B	S	S	
5 AWARDS									
KONOCTI WINERY '89, Clear Lake, Estate $14.00			S			B	S	B	B
4 AWARDS									
LAKEWOOD VINEYARDS '90, California $15.00		G	S			G		G	
VICHON WINERY '90, Napa Vly., Chevrignon $9.60			S	B	B		B		
3 AWARDS									
BAILY VINEYARD '91, Temecula, Montage $11.00						S	G		S
BENZIGER OF GLEN ELLEN '90, Sonoma Mtn., A Tribute $17.00		B	G						S
DE LORIMIER WINERY '90, Alexander Vly., Spectrum $9.00		S						S	B
GEYSER PEAK WINERY '91, Alexander Vly., Chateau Alexandre $13.00		S		G		B			
RABBIT RIDGE VINEYARDS '90, Sonoma Co., Mystique $7.00					B		B	B	
2 AWARDS									
CHATEAU JULIEN WINERY '90, Monterey Co., Platinum $10.00			B	B					
CRESTON VINEYARDS '91, Paso Robles, Estate, Chevrier Blanc $9.00		B					G		
ELLISTON VINEYARDS '91, Sunol Vly. Vnyd., Triomphe $10.00				B		B			
ESTANCIA VINEYARDS '90, Monterey, Estancia Estates $12.00		B		B					
MERRYVALE VINEYARDS '91, Napa Vly. $12.00		G		B					

White Meritage

San Diego	W. Coast	Nat'l O.S.	State Fair	Dallas	San Fran	Farmers	Orange	L.A.	
									2 AWARDS
			B				S		**RABBIT RIDGE VINEYARDS** '91, Sonoma Co., Mystique $7.00
	S	G							**TOPAZ WINES** '89, Napa Vly., SSLH $8.50

DE LOACH

SONOMA COUNTY
RUSSIAN RIVER VALLEY

WHITE-ZINFANDEL

1991

ALCOHOL 12.0% BY VOLUME

Castoro Cellars

San Luis Obispo County

White-Zinfandel

1991

"The Wine"

A fresh wine full of all the fruit this versatile grape offers. This is definitely a wine to enjoy now for any reason, sipping, picnicking, or along with your favorite meals.

PRODUCED AND BOTTLED BY CASTORO WINES
SAN MIGUEL, CALIFORNIA · ALCOHOL 10.5% BY VOLUME

White Zinfandel

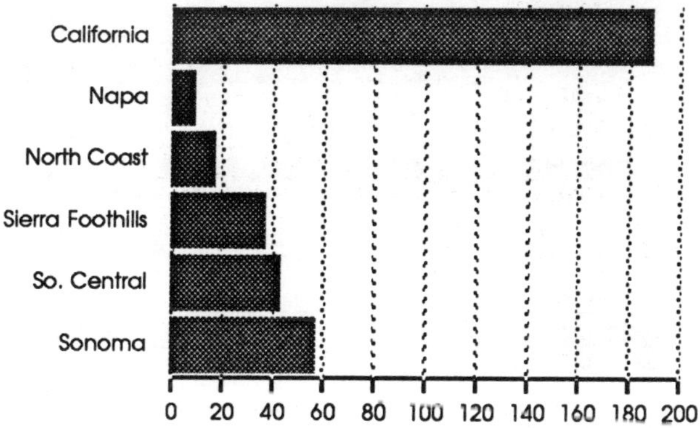

Regional Comparison of Total Points

(Gold=5 Silver=3 Bronze=1)

Highest individual wine totals

21 **DE LOACH VINEYARDS**
'91, Russian River Vly. $9.00

19 **V. SATTUI WINERY**
'91, California $7.50

18 **CASTORO CELLARS**
'91, San Luis Obispo Co. $6.00

17 **GLEN ELLEN WINERY**
'91, California, Prop. Reserve $5.00

14 **M. G. VALLEJO WINERY**
'91, California $4.75

12 **BERINGER VINEYARDS**
'91, North Coast $6.00

9 **WINDSOR VINEYARDS**
'91, Sonoma Co. $7.00

8 **FOREST LAKE VINEYARD**
'90, California $5.00

8 **MONTPELLIER VINEYARDS**
'91, California $6.00

8 **WENTE BROS.**
'91, California, Wente Family Selection $6.00

8 **J. PEDRONCELLI WINERY**
'91, Sonoma Co. $5.50

White Zinfandel

	L.A.	Orange	Farmers	San Fran	Dallas	State Fair	Nat'l O.S.	W. Coast	San Diego
7 AWARDS									
DE LOACH VINEYARDS '91, Russian River Vly. $9.00		S		S	G	B	S	B	G
6 AWARDS									
CASTORO CELLARS '91, San Luis Obispo Co. $6.00		B	S			S	G	S	S
M. G. VALLEJO WINERY '91, California $4.75	S	G	B		B	B	S		
5 AWARDS									
GLEN ELLEN WINERY '91, California, Prop. Reserve $5.00		G			S	S	S		S
V. SATTUI WINERY '91, California $7.50	G		B			G	G		S
4 AWARDS									
BERINGER VINEYARDS '91, North Coast $6.00	G	G			B		B		
E. & J. GALLO '91, California $5.00		B	S				B	B	
MONTPELLIER VINEYARDS '91, California $6.00		B	G	B				B	
J. PEDRONCELLI WINERY '91, Sonoma Co. $5.50	S		B				B	S	
3 AWARDS									
AMADOR FOOTHILL WINERY '91, Amador Co. $5.25	B	G	B						
BARON HERZOG WINE CELLARS '91, California						B	B	B	
CORBETT CANYON VINEYARDS '91, California, Coastal Classic $5.00							B	B	B
CRESTON VINEYARDS '91, Paso Robles $6.00							B	B	B
J. PATRICK DORE WINES '91, California, Floral Series $4.00		G					B		B
ESTRELLA RIVER '91, California, Prop. Res. $5.00	S		S					B	
MILAT VINEYARDS '91, Napa Vly., Estate $6.25			B				B		S
J. PEDRONCELLI WINERY '91, Sonoma Co., Rose $5.50			B			S		S	

White Zinfandel

San Diego	W. Coast	Nat'l O.S.	State Fair	Dallas	San Fran	Farmers	Orange	L.A.	Winery
									3 AWARDS
	G	B						B	**R. H. PHILLIPS VINEYARD** '91, California, Night Harvest $5.00
	B		B					B	**STONE CREEK CELLARS** '91, California $5.00
	S		S		B				**VALLEY OF THE MOON WINERY** '91, Sonoma Vly. $5.00
	S					S	S		**WINDSOR VINEYARDS** '91, Sonoma Co. $7.00
									2 AWARDS
		B						B	**BANDIERA WINERY** '91, California $4.50
B		S							**BEL ARBORS** '90, California, Founders Selection $5.00
							G	B	**CHRISTIAN BROTHERS** '91, California $4.50
	B						S		**DEER VALLEY VINEYARDS** '91, California
		S				S			**DELICATO VINEYARDS** '91, California $4.25
	S							G	**FOREST LAKE VINEYARD** '90, California $5.00
		S		B					**GARLAND RANCH** '91, California
						S	S		**HARMONY CELLARS** '91, Paso Robles $5.75
		S					B		**MIRASSOU VINEYARDS** '91, California $5.50
	G	B							**MOUNT PALOMAR WINERY** '91, Temecula
		S					S		**SANTINO WINES** '91, Amador Co., White Harvest $6.00
					S		B		**STEVENOT WINERY** '91, Amador Co. $5.00
		B					G		**STONY RIDGE WINERY** '91, California
	S					B			**TWIN HILLS RANCH WINERY** '91, Paso Robles $5.25
							S	G	**WENTE BROS.** '91, California, Wente Family Select. $6.00

GREENWOOD
RIDGE
VINEYARDS

SONOMA COUNTY
ZINFANDEL
1990

SCHERRER VINEYARDS

ALCOHOL 13.0% BY VOLUME

DE LOACH

SONOMA COUNTY
RUSSIAN RIVER VALLEY
ZINFANDEL
ESTATE BOTTLED
1990

ALCOHOL 13.7% BY VOLUME

Zinfandel

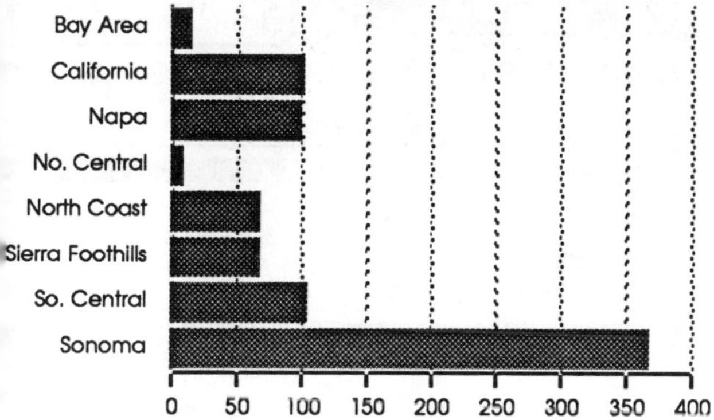

Regional Comparison of Total Points

(Gold=5 Silver=3 Bronze=1)

Highest individual wine totals

26 **GREENWOOD RIDGE VINEYARDS**
'90, Sonoma Co., Scherrer Vnyd. $12.50

20 **FETZER VINEYARDS**
'89, California, Barrel Select $9.00

19 **VILLA MT. EDEN WINERY**
'90, California, Cellar Select $9.00

17 **DE LOACH VINEYARDS**
'90, Russian River Vly., Estate $11.50

16 **PEACHY CANYON WINERY**
'89, Paso Robles $10.00

16 **GARY FARRELL WINES**
'90, Russian River Vly., Collins Vnyd. $14.00

16 **ROSENBLUM CELLARS**
'90, Sonoma Co. $12.00

15 **DAVID BRUCE WINERY**
'90, San Luis Obispo Co. $12.00

14 **BEL ARBORS**
'90, California, Founders Selection $5.00

Zinfandel

Zinfandel	L.A.	Orange	Farmers	San Fran	Dallas	State Fair	Nat'l O.S.	W. Coast	San Diego
8 AWARDS									
GREENWOOD RIDGE VINEYARDS '90, Sonoma Co., Scherrer Vnyd. $12.50	B	S	S	G	B	S	G	G	
7 AWARDS									
DE LOACH VINEYARDS '90, Russian River Vly., Estate $11.50		B	B		S	S	G	S	B
VILLA MT. EDEN WINERY '90, California, Cellar Select $9.00		B	B	G		B	G	G	B
6 AWARDS									
BEL ARBORS '90, California, Founders Selection $5.00	B			B	S	B	G		S
CASTORO CELLARS '90, Paso Robles $9.00		B	B	B		B		S	B
FETZER VINEYARDS '89, California, Barrel Select $9.00	S	S		S	S		G	S	
HAYWOOD WINERY '90, Sonoma Vly., Los Chamizal Vnyd. $14.00	B	B	B	B				B	[illegible]
MARK WEST VINEYARDS '89, Sonoma Co., Robert Rue Vnyd. $17.00		B	G	S		B		B	[illegible]
5 AWARDS									
BENZIGER OF GLEN ELLEN '89, Sonoma Co. $10.00	B	S	B	G		S			
FRANCISCAN OAKVILLE ESTATE '90, Napa Vly. $13.00	B	S				B	G	S	
V. SATTUI WINERY '89, Napa Vly., Suzanne's Vnyd., Estate $12.75			S	B		S	B		[illegible]
4 AWARDS									
ARCIERO WINERY '88, Paso Robles $7.49			B		B			B	
AUDUBON CELLARS '90, Sonoma Co., Passenger Pigeon $12.00	B	S		S		S			
BOEGER WINERY '89, Napa Vly., Nichelini Vnyd. $12.00			B	B			B		
CRESTON VINEYARDS '90, Paso Robles, Estate $9.75			B	B	B		B		
ELIZABETH VINEYARDS '90, Mendocino $10.00		G		B		B		B	

Zinfandel

San Dego	W. Coast	Nat'l O.S.	State Fair	Dallas	San Fran	Farmers	Orange	L.A.	
4 AWARDS									
	G		G		G	B			**GARY FARRELL WINES** '90, Russian River Vly., Collins Vnyd. $14.00
			S		B	B	B		**GUENOC WINERY** '89, California $9.50
G					S	S		B	**HIDDEN CELLARS** '89, Mendocino Co., Pacini Vnyd. $10.00
	S		S		G		B		**LIMERICK LANE** '90, Russian River Vly. $10.00
B					S	G	S		**LOLONIS WINERY** '90, Mendocino Co., Reserve $12.00
S	S			S		S			**LYTTON SPRINGS WINERY** '89, Sonoma Co. $15.00
		S				S	B	B	**ORGANIC WINE WORKS** '91, California, LH $8.50
S		S		G		G			**PEACHY CANYON WINERY** '89, Paso Robles $10.00
B	G					B	G		**QUIVIRA VINEYARDS** '90, Dry Creek Vly. $12.75
B	G				S			S	**A. RAFANELLI WINERY** '90, Dry Creek Vly. $12.00
	G		B		G		G		**ROSENBLUM CELLARS** '90, Sonoma Co. $12.00
		S	B		S		B		**ROUND HILL CELLARS** '89, Napa Vly. $6.00
B	B		B			S			**RODNEY STRONG VINEYARDS** '88, River West Vnyd., Old Vines, Estate $14.00
G					S	S		B	**WINDSOR VINEYARDS** '88, Dry Creek Vly., Reserve $10.00
			S		B	B		B	**WINDSOR VINEYARDS** '87, Russian River Vly., Blackberry Ranch $11.00
3 AWARDS									
G				B		B			**ADELAIDA CELLARS** '89, Paso Robles $12.00
	G				G	G			**DAVID BRUCE WINERY** '90, San Luis Obispo Co. $12.00

Zinfandel

3 AWARDS	L.A.	Orange	Farmers	San Fran	Dallas	State Fair	Nat'l O.S.	W. Coast	San Diego
BUEHLER VINEYARDS '89, Napa Vly. $9.50			B	B				S	
DAVIS BYNUM WINERY '90, Russian River Vly. $11.00				G		B		S	
CHATEAU SOUVERAIN '89, Dry Creek Vly. $7.50			B	B		B			
CLOS DU VAL '88, Napa Vly., Stags Leap Dist., Estate $14.00		B		B		B			
EAGLE RIDGE WINERY '89, Amador Co., Grand Pere Vnyd. $12.00			B			B			B
EBERLE WINERY '90, Paso Robles, Sauret Vnyd. $12.00		B						G	B
GRANITE SPRINGS WINERY '89, El Dorado, Higgins Vnyd. $12.00	G			G		S			
GRGICH HILLS CELLAR '88, Sonoma $12.00	B		G						B
GUGLIELMO WINERY '88, Santa Clara Vly., Estate Reserve $8.00	G			B					B
GUNDLACH-BUNDSCHU '90, Sonoma Vly., Rhinefarm Vnyd., Estate $10.00		S		S		S			
HOP KILN WINERY '90, Sonoma Co. $12.00		B		B		G			
IMAGERY SERIES '90, Dry Creek Vly., LH $16.00		S	S				S		
TOBIN JAMES '90, Paso Robles, Blue Moon Reserve $12.00		B		B				S	
MIRASSOU VINEYARDS 'NV, California, Lot 6 $5.50	B	B	B						
RABBIT RIDGE VINEYARDS '90, Dry Creek Vly. $10.00					G		S	G	
RICHARDSON VINEYARDS '90, Sonoma Vly. $11.00		B	B					G	
ROSENBLUM CELLARS '90, Contra Costa Co. $10.00		B		B			B		
SANTA BARBARA WINERY '91, Central Coast, Beaujour $8.00		B		B	B				

Zinfandel

San Diego	W. Coast	Nat'l O.S.	State Fair	Dallas	San Fran	Farmers	Orange	L.A.	Zinfandel
									3 AWARDS
			S	B			G		**SAUCELITO CANYON** '90, Arroyo Grande Vly., Estate $12.00
		B				B	S		**SEGHESIO WINERY** '89, Sonoma Co. $7.50
	S	B		S					**SONORA WINERY** '90, Sonoma Co. $9.00
B	B					S			**STORYBOOK MT. VINEYARDS** '88, Napa Vly., Estate, Reserve $19.50
B	S		B						**VALLEY RIDGE** '88, Sonoma Co. $7.00
	B		S			B			**WHITE OAK VINEYARDS** '89, Sonoma Vly. $12.95
									2 AWARDS
					B	S			**AMADOR FOOTHILL WINERY** '89, Shenandoah, Ferrero Vnyd. $10.00
					S	B			**AMADOR FOOTHILL WINERY** '89, Shenandoah, Grand Pere $10.00
	S		B						**BARON HERZOG WINE CELLARS** '90, Sonoma Co.
							G	G	**BELVEDERE WINERY** '90, Dry Creek Vly. $10.00
		S				B			**BELVEDERE WINERY** '89, Dry Creek Vly. $10.00
			B		S				**BERINGER VINEYARDS** '89, Napa Co. $8.00
B						B			**BERINGER VINEYARDS** '88, North Coast $8.50
			B		B				**BOEGER WINERY** '90, El Dorado, Walker Vnyd. $10.00
					B			S	**BRANDBORG CELLARS** '90, Mt. Veeder $11.00
		S	B						**BURGESS CELLARS** '89, Napa Vly.
G		B							**CAYMUS VINEYARDS** '89, Napa Vly.
S		B							**CHESTNUT HILL** '89, San Luis Obispo Co. $6.00

Zinfandel	L.A.	Orange	Farmers	San Fran	Dallas	State Fair	Nat'l O.S.	W. Coast	San Diego
2 AWARDS									
CLINE CELLARS '90, Contra Costa Co. $9.00						B		G	
DRY CREEK VINEYARD '89, Dry Creek Vly. $11.00					S		B		
EAGLE RIDGE WINERY '89, Amador Co., Grand Pere Vnyd., LH $9.50			B				B		
EBERLE WINERY '89, Paso Robles $12.00					B		S		
FENESTRA WINERY '89, Livermore Vly.				B					S
FIELDBROOK VALLEY WINERY '91, Mendocino, Pacini Vnyd. $11.00		G				S			
GRANITE SPRINGS WINERY '89, El Dorado, Twin Rivers Vnyd.	S					B			
HOWELL MOUNTAIN VINEYARDS '88, Napa Vly.	B								S
TOBIN JAMES '89, Paso Robles, Inspiration $12.00				G	B				
JANKRIS VINEYARD '89, Paso Robles $8.75			S			G			
KENDALL-JACKSON WINERY '88, Anderson Vly., DuPratt Vnyd. $20.00			S				S		
KENDALL-JACKSON WINERY '88, Mendocino, Ciapusci Vnyd. $20.00			B				S		
KENWOOD VINEYARDS '90, Sonoma Co., Jack London Vnyd. $14.00				B		S			
KENWOOD VINEYARDS '89, Sonoma Vly., Jack London Vnyd. $14.00			B						B
LAVA CAP WINERY '89, El Dorado, Estate $8.50						B		B	
LOLONIS WINERY '89, Mendocino Co., Lot 2, Reserve $10.00					B				B
MADRONA VINEYARDS '89, El Dorado, Madrona Vnyd. $8.50			B			B			
LOUIS M. MARTINI WINERY '88, Sonoma/Napa Co. $8.00	B		B						

Zinfandel

2 AWARDS

San Diego	W. Coast	Nat'l O.S.	State Fair	Dallas	San Fran	Farmers	Orange	L.A.	Zinfandel
			S			G			**MEEKER VINEYARD** '89, Dry Creek Vly., Estate $10.00
			B		B				**MONTEVINA WINES** '89, Amador Co. $9.00
	S						B		**NEVADA CITY WINERY** '90, Sierra Foothills $6.00
			S		B				**RAVENSWOOD** '89, Sonoma Co. $11.00
			S				G		**ROSENBLUM CELLARS** 'NV, California, Vintner's Cuvee V $7.50
			B		S				**SANTINO WINES** '89, Shenandoah Vly., Grandpere $12.00
		B	B						**SANTINO WINES** '89, Amador Co., Grand Pere Vnyd.
S						B			**V. SATTUI WINERY** '88, Napa Vly., Howell Mtn. $13.00
S		B							**V. SATTUI WINERY** '87, Napa Vly., Howell Mtn. Reserve $13.00
			S		S				**SEGHESIO WINERY** '90, Sonoma Co. $8.00
			B		B				**STORYBOOK MT. VINEYARDS** '90, Napa Vly. $14.00
B								B	**SUMMIT LAKE VINEYARDS** '88, Howell Mtn., Estate
					B			S	**TRENTADUE** '90, Alexander Vly. $10.00
B			B						**WILDHURST VINEYARDS** '90, Clear Lake

ALL VARIETALS

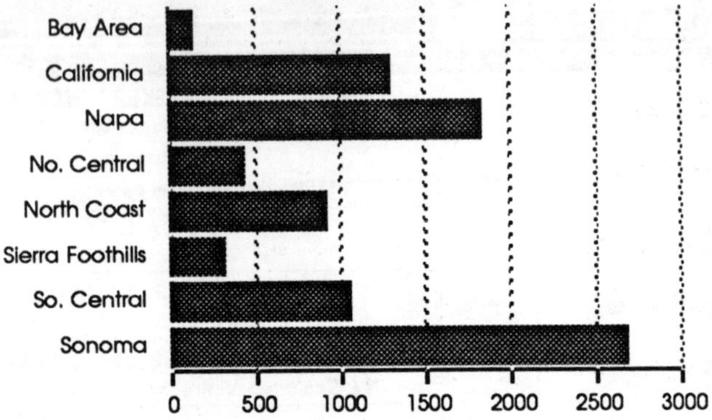

Regional Comparison of Total Points

(Gold=5 Silver=3 Bronze=1)

Highest individual wine totals

220 **WINDSOR VINEYARDS**
11455 Old Redwood Hwy., Healdsburg CA

157 **GEYSER PEAK WINERY**
22281 Chianti Rd., Geyserville CA 95441

154 **GUENOC WINERY**
21000 Butts Canyon Rd., Middletown CA

145 **FETZER VINEYARDS**
13325 So. Highway 101, Hopland CA

139 **KENDALL-JACKSON WINERY**
640 Mathews Rd., Lakeport CA 95453

130 **BENZIGER OF GLEN ELLEN**
1883 London Ranch Rd., Glen Ellen CA

105 **NAVARRO VINEYARDS**
5601 Highway 128, Philo CA 95466

102 **DE LOACH VINEYARDS**
1791 Olivet Rd., Santa Rosa CA 95401

94 **GREENWOOD RIDGE VINEYARDS**
24555 Greenwood Rd., Philo CA 95466

88 **BERINGER VINEYARDS**
2000 Main Street, St Helena CA 94574

87 **MIRASSOU VINEYARDS**
3000 Aborn Rd., San Jose CA 95135

83 **V. SATTUI WINERY**
1111 White Lane, St Helena CA 94574

77 **GARY FARRELL WINES**
P. O. Box 342, Forestville CA 95436

76 **DAVID BRUCE WINERY**
21439 Bear Creek Rd., Los Gatos CA

76 **CLOS DU BOIS**
5 Fitch Street, Healdsburg CA 95448

76 **DRY CREEK VINEYARD**
3770 Lambert Bridge, Healdsburg CA

76 **HUSCH VINEYARDS**
4400 Highway 128, Philo CA 95466

75 **CHATEAU ST. JEAN**
8555 Sonoma Hwy., Kenwood CA 95452

70 **RODNEY STRONG VINEYARDS**
11455 Old Redwood Hwy., Windsor CA

68 **VILLA MT. EDEN WINERY**
620 Oakville Cross Rd., Oakville CA 94562

65 **CULBERTSON WINERY**
2608 Via Rancheros, Fallbrook CA 92028

63 **HANDLEY CELLARS**
P. O. Box 66, Philo CA 95466

62 **LOCKWOOD VINEYARD**
1044 Harkins Road, Salinas CA 93901

61 **BYRON VINEYARD**
5230 Tepusquet Rd., Santa Maria CA

59 **CASTORO CELLARS**
1480 No. Bethel Road, Templeton CA

59 **ST. CLEMENT VINEYARDS**
2867 St. Helena Hwy. N., St Helena CA

57 **MUMM NAPA VALLEY**
1111 Dunaweal Ln., Calistoga CA 94515

57 **VICHON WINERY**
1595 Oakville Grade, Oakville CA 94562

56 **LOUIS M. MARTINI WINERY**
254 St. Helena Hwy., N., St Helena CA

53 **BEL ARBORS**
13325 So. Highway 101, Hopland CA

53 **BUENA VISTA WINERY**
27000 Ramal Road, Sonoma CA 95476

53 **PARDUCCI WINE CELLARS**
501 Parducci Rd., Ukiah CA 95482

ABBEY D'OR

4620 Hog Canyon Rd. San Miguel 93451

Cabernet Sauvignon,'87, Paso Robles (2)

ACACIA

2750 Las Amigas Road Napa 94558

Chardonnay,'90, Napa Vly., Carneros (2)
Pinot Noir,'90, Napa Vly., Carneros (S-Orange)

ADELAIDA CELLARS

2170 Adelaida Star Rd. Paso Robles 93446

Cabernet Sauvignon,'88, Paso Robles $14.50 (2)
Chardonnay,'90, Paso Robles (2)
Zinfandel,'89, Paso Robles $12.00 (3)

ADLER FELS WINERY

5325 Corrick Lane Santa Rosa 95405

Gewurztraminer,'90, Sonoma Co., Estate $9.00 (2)
Gewurztraminer,'91, Sonoma Co. $9.00 (6)
Sauvignon Blanc,'90, Sonoma Co., Fume $9.00 (3)

ALDERBROOK WINERY

2306 Magnolia Drive Healdsburg 95448

Chardonnay,'90, Dry Creek Vly. $11.00 (2)
Sauvignon Blanc,'90, Dry Creek Vly., Estate $8.00 (3)

ALEXANDER VALLEY FRUIT & TRADING

5110 Highway 128 Geyserville 95441

Zinfandel,'90, Alexander Vly., LH (B-Orange)
Zinfandel,'90, Alexander Vly., Sommer Vnyds (S-Nat'l O.S.)

ALEXANDER VALLEY VINEYARDS

8644 Highway 128 Healdsburg 95448

Cabernet Sauvignon,'88, Alex. Vly., Wetzel Vnyd. $13.00 (B-Dallas)
Chenin Blanc,'90, Alexander Vly., Wetzel Vnyd. (2)
Gewurztraminer,'91, Alexander Vly., Wetzel Vnyd. (2)
Johannisberg Riesling,'91, Alexander Vly., Wetzel Vnyd.
Merlot,'89, Alexander Vly., Wetzel Vnyd. $14.00 (S-Orange)
Pinot Noir,'89, Alexander Vly., Wetzel Vnyd. (B-Orange)

ALMADEN VINEYARDS

1530 Blossom Hill Rd. San Jose 95118

Sauvignon Blanc,'NV, California (S-Orange)
White Zinfandel,'NV, California (S-Orange)
White Zinfandel,'NV, California, Light (S-Orange)

AMADOR FOOTHILL WINERY

12500 Steiner Road Plymouth 95669

Sauvignon Blanc,'90, Shenandoah Vly., Fume (B-Nat'l O.S.)
White Zinfandel,'91, Amador Co. $5.25 (3)
Zinfandel,'89, Shenandoah, Ferrero Vnyd. $10.00 (2)
Zinfandel,'89, Shenandoah, Grand Pere $10.00 (2)

S. ANDERSON VINEYARD

1473 Yountville Creek Rd. Napa 94558

Chardonnay,'88, Napa Vly., Stag's Leap (B-W. Coast)
Sparkling Wine,'86, Napa Vly., Brut $20.00 (2)
Sparkling Wine,'87, Napa Vly., Blanc De Noirs $20.00 (4)

ANGELS CREEK

Address not available

Chardonnay,'88, California (?)

ANTELOPE VALLEY WINERY

P. O. Box 833 Leona Valley 93551

Zinfandel,'90, Antelope Vly., Godde Vnyd. (B-Nat'l O.S.)

APTOS VINEYARD

4390 Hecker Pass Road Gilroy 95020

Pinot Noir,'89, Santa Cruz Co. $11.95 (2)

ARCIERO WINERY

P. O. Box 1287 Paso Robles 93447

Chardonnay,'89, Paso Robles, Estate $8.69 (3)
Petite Sirah,'87, Paso Robles, Estate $7.00 (2)
Zinfandel,'88, Paso Robles $7.49 (4)

ARMIDA WINERY

2201 Westside Road Healdsburg 95448

Chardonnay,'90, Russian River Vly. (2)

ARROWOOD VINEYARDS

P. O. Box 987 Glen Ellen 95442

Cabernet Sauvignon,'88, Sonoma Co. (2)

VINCENT ARROYO WINERY

2361 Greenwood Ave. Calistoga 94515

Petite Sirah,'89, Napa Vly., Estate (B-San Diego)

AU BON CLIMAT

Address not available

Pinot Noir,'89, Santa Ynez, Benedict Vnyd. (B-Orange)

AUDUBON CELLARS

600 Addison Street Berkeley 94710

Cabernet Sauvignon,'90, Napa Vly. (2)
Sauvignon Blanc,'89, Napa Vly. (2)
Zinfandel,'90, Sonoma Co., Passenger Pigeon $12.00 (4)

AUSTIN CELLARS

P. O. Box 636 Los Olivos 93441

Johannisberg Riesling,'90, Santa Barbara Co. $7.50 (3)
Pinot Noir,'88, Santa Barbara Co., Reserve $25.00 (B-Farmers)
White Meritage,'89, Santa Barbara Co., Cumulus (G-Nat'l O.S.)

B

AILY VINEYARD

36150 Pauba Road Temecula 92390

Johannisberg Riesling,'91, Temecula, Wickets Vnyd. $7.95 (3)
White Meritage,'91, Temecula, Montage $11.00 (3)

ALLATORE CHAMPAGNE

P. O. Box 1130 Modesto 95353

Sparkling Wine,'NV, California, Gran Spumante $5.50 (8)

ANCROFT

Address not available

Chardonnay,'90, Napa Vly., Howell Mtn. (B-Orange)

BANDIERA WINERY

155 Cherry Creek Rd. Cloverdale 95425

Cabernet Sauvignon,'88, Napa Vly. $6.50 (3)
Sauvignon Blanc,'90, Napa Co. $5.00 (2)
White Zinfandel,'91, California $4.50 (2)

BANNISTER

Address not available

Chardonnay,'90, Russian River (B-Orange)

BAREFOOT CELLARS

8075-B Westside Road Healdsburg 95448

Cabernet Sauvignon,'NV, California $5.00 (5)
Chardonnay,'NV, California $5.00 (2)
Sauvignon Blanc,'NV, California $5.00 (3)

BARGETTO WINERY

3535 N. Main Street Soquel 95073

Cabernet Sauvignon,'86, Santa Cruz Mtns. $18.00 (S-L.A.)
Chardonnay,'90, Central Coast, Cypress $9.00 (4)
Chardonnay,'90, Santa Cruz Mtns. $18.00 (3)
Gewurztraminer,'91, Monterey Co. $8.00 (5)
Pinot Noir,'87, Santa Maria Vly. $16.00 (S-San Diego)
Pinot Noir,'88, Santa Maria Vly. $16.00 (S-L.A.)
Sauvignon Blanc,'91, California (B-Orange)

BARON HERZOG WINE CELLARS

12378 Saratoga-Sunnyvale Rd. Saratoga 95070

Cabernet Sauvignon,'86, Sonoma Co., Reserve $15.00 (B-Farmers)
Cabernet Sauvignon,'90, California Selection (B-Orange)
Chardonnay,'90, California $10.75 (B-W. Coast)
Chenin Blanc,'91, California $5.25 (G-Farmers)
Johannisberg Riesling,'90, Monterey Co., LH $15.00 (2)
Johannisberg Riesling,'91, Monterey Co., LH $15.00 (3)
Sauvignon Blanc,'90, Sonoma Co. (S-Nat'l O.S.)
Sauvignon Blanc,'91, California $9.00 (2)
White Zinfandel,'91, California (3)
Zinfandel,'90, Sonoma Co. (2)
Zinfandel,'91, Sonoma, Special Cuvee $12.00 (B-San Fran)

BEAULIEU VINEYARD

1960 St. Helena Highway Rutherford 94573

Cabernet Sauvignon,'87, Napa Co., Geo. De Latou $37.00 (3)
Cabernet Sauvignon,'89, Napa Vly., Beautour $9.00 (B-Orange)
Cabernet Sauvignon,'89, Napa Vly., Rutherford, Estate (2)
Chardonnay,'89, Napa Vly., Carneros Reserve $17.00 (4)
Chardonnay,'90, Napa Vly., Beautour $9.00 (B-Orange)
Pinot Noir,'89, Carneros, Reserve (B-L.A.)
Pinot Noir,'90, Napa Vly., Estate $9.00 (B-Orange)
Sauvignon Blanc,'89, Napa Vly., Beautour Fume $7.75 (3)
Sauvignon Blanc,'90, Napa Vly., Estate (B-Orange)

BEL ARBORS

13325 So. Highway 101 Hopland 95449

Cabernet Sauvignon,'NV, American, Cask 89 (G-San Diego)
Chardonnay,'NV, American, Cask 90 (B-San Diego)
Merlot,'90, California $5.00 (2)
Merlot,'NV, American Grown, Cask 89 (2)
Sauvignon Blanc,'90, California, Founders Selection $5.00 (4)

White Zinfandel,'90, California, Founders Selection $5.00 (2)
White Zinfandel,'91, California $5.00 (B-San Fran)
Zinfandel,'90, California, Founders Selection $5.00 (6)

BELVEDERE WINERY

4035 Westside Road Healdsburg 95448

Chardonnay,'90, Alexander Vly. (B-Orange)
Chardonnay,'90, Russian River Vly. $13.00 (5)
Chardonnay,'90, Sonoma Co., Preferred Stock $18.00 (4)
Zinfandel,'89, Dry Creek Vly. $10.00 (2)
Zinfandel,'90, Dry Creek Vly. $10.00 (2)

BENZIGER OF GLEN ELLEN

1883 London Ranch Rd. Glen Ellen 95442

Cabernet Sauvignon,'89, Sonoma Co. $12.00 (6)
Cabernet Sauvignon,'89, Sonoma Mtn., Estate (2)
Chardonnay,'90, Carneros, Premiere Vnyd. (2)
Chardonnay,'90, Sonoma Co. $12.00 (5)
Merlot,'89, Sonoma Co. $14.00 (5)
Merlot,'89, Sonoma Mtn., Estate Bottled $20.00 (2)
Red Meritage,'88, Sonoma Mtn., A Tribute (B-Nat'l O.S.)
Red Meritage,'89, Sonoma Mtn., A Tribute $25.00 (5)
Sauvignon Blanc,'90, Sonoma Co. Fume $9.00 (3)
Sauvignon Blanc,'90, Sonoma Mtn., Estate $14.00 (2)
Sparkling Wine,'88, Carneros, Brut, Blanc De Blancs $14.00 (5)
White Meritage,'90, Sonoma Mtn., A Tribute $17.00 (3)
Zinfandel,'89, Sonoma Co. $10.00 (5)

BERGFELD WINERY

401 St. Helena Hwy., So. St Helena 94574

Cabernet Sauvignon,'88, Napa Vly., Estate $15.00 (G-Orange)
Cabernet Sauvignon,'89, Napa Vly. $15.00 (B-San Fran)
Sauvignon Blanc,'90, Napa Vly. $9.00 (B-San Fran)

BERINGER VINEYARDS

2000 Main Street St Helena 94574

Cabernet Sauvignon,'86, Napa, Chabot Vnyd. $35.00 (S-State Fair)
Cabernet Sauvignon,'87, Napa Vly. $14.00 (G-State Fair)
Cabernet Sauvignon,'88, Knight's Vly., Prop. $16.00 (G-Dallas)
Cabernet Sauvignon,'89, Knight's Vly., Proprietor Grown $16.00 (3)
Chardonnay,'90, Napa Vly., Prop Grown, Reserve $19.00 (5)
Chardonnay,'90, Napa Vly., Prop. Grown $12.00 (5)
Chenin Blanc,'90, Napa Vly. $6.00 (2)
Chenin Blanc,'91, Napa Vly. $7.50 (3)
Gewurztraminer,'90, Napa Vly. (B-Nat'l O.S.)
Gewurztraminer,'91, North Coast $7.50 (2)
Johannisberg Riesling,'89, North Coast (B-Orange)
Johannisberg Riesling,'90, North Coast $7.50 (3)
Sauvignon Blanc,'90, Knights Vly., Prop. Grown $9.00 (S-Farmers)
Sauvignon Blanc,'90, Napa Vly., Fume $8.00 (B-Dallas)
White Zinfandel,'91, North Coast $6.00 (4)
Zinfandel,'88, North Coast $8.50 (2)
Zinfandel,'89, Napa Co. $8.00 (2)

BLACK MOUNTAIN VINEYARD

101 Grant Ave. Healdsburg 95448

Cabernet Sauvignon,'88, Alexander Vly., Fat Cat $18.00 (4)
Cabernet Sauvignon,'89, California (B-W. Coast)
Chardonnay,'88, Alexander Vly., Gravel Bar $18.00 (3)

Petite Sirah,'88, Alexander Vly., Bosun Crest $9.00 (3)
White Zinfandel,'88, Cramer Ridge (G-L.A.)

BLACK SHEEP VINTNERS

634 French Gulch Rd. Murphys 95247

Cabernet Sauvignon,'89, Sierra Foothills $12.00 (B-State Fair)

BLOSSOM HILL COLLECTION

P. O. Box 391 St Helena 94574

Merlot,'NV, California, Reserve Cask (B-Orange)
Sauvignon Blanc,'90, California (B-Orange)

BOEGER WINERY

1709 Carson Road Placerville 95667

Cabernet Sauvignon,'87, El Dorado (B-State Fair)
Chardonnay,'90, Part Barrel Ferm. (B-L.A.)
Merlot,'89, El Dorado, Estate (2)
Sauvignon Blanc,'90, El Dorado, Estate (S-Orange)
Zinfandel,'89, Napa Vly., Nichelini Vnyd. $12.00 (4)
Zinfandel,'90, El Dorado, Walker Vnyd. $10.00 (2)

BOGLE VINEYARDS

Rt. 1, Box 276 Clarksburg 95612

Cabernet Sauvignon,'90, California $6.00 (B-State Fair)
Chardonnay,'91, California $6.00 (4)
Merlot,'90, California $6.00 (2)
Petite Sirah,'90, California $6.00 (2)
Sauvignon Blanc,'91, California, Fume $6.00 (S-San Diego)
White Zinfandel,'91, California $6.00 (B-Farmers)

BON JORY

Address not available

Pinot Noir,'89, Santa Clara Vly., San Ysidro (B-Orange)

BON MARCHE

820 Greenfield Rd. St Helena 94574

Pinot Noir,'91, Sonoma Co. $8.00 (4)

BOUCHAINE VINEYARDS

1975 Buchli Sta. Rd. Napa 94558

Chardonnay,'88, Carneros, Estate Reserve $21.00 (B-San Diego)
Chardonnay,'90, Napa Vly. $15.00 (2)
Gewurztraminer,'90, Russian River Vly., Dry $8.50 (2)
Pinot Noir,'89, Napa Vly, Carneros $15.00 (2)

BOYER WINERY

P. O. Box 842 Soledad 93960

Chardonnay,'90, Monterey Co., Ventana Vnyd. (G-Nat'l O.S.)

BRANDBORG CELLARS

Address not available

Pinot Noir,'90, Bien Nacido Vnyd. $13.00 (2)
Pinot Noir,'90, Mendocino Co. (B-State Fair)
Zinfandel,'90, Mt. Veeder $11.00 (2)

BRANDER VINEYARD

P. O. Box 92 Los Olivos 93441

Red Meritage,'89, Bouchet Tete De Cuvee $20.00 (3)
Sauvignon Blanc,'90, Santa Ynez, Tete De Cuvee $9.75 (2)

BRAREN PAULI WINERY

1613 Spring Hill Rd Petaluma 94952

Cabernet Sauvignon,'88, Mendocino Co. $13.00 (B-Dallas)
Cabernet Sauvignon,'89, Dry Creek, Mauritson $13.00 (S-San Fran)
Merlot,'89, Alexander Vly., Mauritson Vnyd. $13.00 (B-Dallas)

BRIARWOOD CELLARS

14653 Titus St. Panorama City 91402

Chardonnay,'91, California (B-State Fair)

BRICELAND VINEYARDS

5959 Briceland Rd. Redway 95560

Sauvignon Blanc,'90, Lake Co., Vina Las Lomas Vnyd. (S-Orange)
Sauvignon Blanc,'90, Mendocino Co. (B-State Fair)
Sparkling Wine,'88, Humboldt Co., Brut (S-Orange)

BRINDIAMO

Address not available

Chardonnay,'90, Temecula, Nelson Vnyd. $10.00 (B-Farmers)
Pinot Noir,'90, Santa Maria Hills Vnyd., Ltd. Btlg. (G-Orange)

DAVID BRUCE WINERY

21439 Bear Creek Rd. Los Gatos 95030

Chardonnay,'90, Santa Cruz Mtns., Estate $18.00 (B-Orange)
Petite Sirah,'90, California, Vintner's Select $10.00 (6)
Pinot Noir,'89, S. Barbara/Sonoma/SLO, Vint. Sel. $12.00 (4)
Pinot Noir,'89, Santa Cruz Mtn., Estate, Reserve $27.00 (3)
Pinot Noir,'89, Santa Cruz Mtns., Estate $22.00 (5)
Zinfandel,'90, San Luis Obispo Co. $12.00 (3)

BRUTACAO CELLARS

2300 Highway 175 Hopland 95445

Cabernet Sauvignon,'88, Mendocino (B-W. Coast)

BUEHLER VINEYARDS

820 Greenfield Rd. St Helena 94574

Chardonnay,'91, Sonoma Co. (B-State Fair)
Zinfandel,'89, Napa Vly. $9.50 (3)

BUENA VISTA WINERY

27000 Ramal Road Sonoma 95476

Cabernet Sauvignon,'88, Carneros, Estate $12.00 (3)
Chardonnay,'89, Carneros, Reserve $17.50 (3)
Chardonnay,'90, Carneros $11.00 (3)
Gewurztraminer,'90, Carneros, Estate $7.50 (G-San Diego)
Gewurztraminer,'91, Carneros $7.50 (3)
Merlot,'88, Carneros, Reserve $18.00 (B-San Diego)
Merlot,'89, Carneros $11.00 (B-W. Coast)
Merlot,'90, Carneros $11.00 (S-Orange)
Pinot Noir,'89, Carneros, Estate $9.00 (2)
Pinot Noir,'90, Carneros $9.00 (B-Orange)
Sauvignon Blanc,'90, Lake Co. $7.00 (2)
Sauvignon Blanc,'91, Lake Co. $7.00 (4)

BURGESS CELLARS

1108 Deer Park Rd. St Helena 94574

Cabernet Sauvignon,'88, Napa Vly., Vintage Selection $19.00 (5)
Chardonnay,'90, Napa Vly., Triere Vnyd. (B-Orange)
Zinfandel,'89, Napa Vly. (2)

BUTTERFLY CREEK WINERY

4063 Bear Creek Road Mariposa 95338

Johannisberg Riesling,'90, Sierra Foothills, White Riesling $9.50 (3)
Merlot,'89, Sierra Foothills, Chaple Vnyd. $15.00 (2)

BYINGTON WINERY

21850 Bear Creek Rd. Los Gatos 95030

Sauvignon Blanc,'90, Monterey Co., Fume (B-Nat'l O.S.)

DAVIS BYNUM WINERY

8075 Westside Rd. Healdsburg 95448

Cabernet Sauvignon,'89, Sonoma Co. $11.00 (2)
Chardonnay,'90, Russian River Vly., Ltd. Release $11.00 (B-Orange)
Gewurztraminer,'91, Russian River $8.00 (4)
Merlot,'89, Sonoma Co., Ltd. Release $12.50 (2)
Merlot,'90, Sonoma Co., Ltd. Release $12.50 (2)
Pinot Noir,'89, Russian River Vly. $12.50 (B-Farmers)
Sauvignon Blanc,'91, Russian River Vly. Fume $8.00 (4)
Zinfandel,'90, Russian River Vly. $11.00 (3)

BYRON VINEYARD

5230 Tepusquet Rd. Santa Maria 93454

Cabernet Sauvignon,'89, Santa Barbara Co. $16.00 (6)
Chardonnay,'89, Paso Robles, Reserve (B-Nat'l O.S.)
Chardonnay,'90, Santa Barbara Co. $14.00 (5)
Chardonnay,'90, Santa Barbara Co., Reserve $18.00 (2)
Pinot Noir,'89, Santa Barbara Co., Reserve $20.00 (2)
Pinot Noir,'90, Santa Barbara Co. $13.00 (2)
Red Meritage,'89, Santa Barbara Co. (B-Orange)
Sauvignon Blanc,'90, Santa Barbara Co. $9.00 (2)
Sauvignon Blanc,'91, Santa Barbara Co. $9.00 (2)
Sparkling Wine,'NV, Santa Barbara, Brut, Res. $18.00 (2)

C

CAIN CELLARS

3800 Langtry Rd. St Helena 94574

Red Meritage,'86, Napa Vly, Cain Five $30.00 (B-Dallas)
Red Meritage,'87, Napa Vly. $30.00 (S-Orange)
Sauvignon Blanc,'90, Carneros, Musque $12.00 (S-San Fran)

CAKEBREAD CELLARS

8300 St. Helena Hwy. Rutherford 94573

Cabernet Sauvignon,'89, Napa Vly. (S-Orange)

CALLAWAY VINEYARD

32720 Rancho California Temecula 92390

Cabernet Sauvignon,'89, California, America's Cup $12.00 (2)
Chenin Blanc,'90, Temecula, Morning Harvest $7.00 (2)
Johannisberg Riesling,'91, Temecula, Seasonal Refuge $7.00 (2)
Sauvignon Blanc,'90, Temecula $8.00 (2)

CAMBRIA WINERY

Route 1, Box 142 Santa Maria 93454

Chardonnay,'89, Santa Maria Vly., Reserve $25.00 (4)
Chardonnay,'90, Santa Maria, Katherine's Vnyd. $16.00 (3)
Pinot Noir,'89, Santa Maria Vly., Julia's Vnyd. $16.00 (5)

CANYON ROAD CELLARS
22281 Chianti Rd. Geyserville 95441
Chardonnay,'91, California $4.00 (4)
White Zinfandel,'91, California $4.00 (S-San Fran)

CAREY CELLARS
1711 Alamo Pintado Rd. Solvang 93463
Cabernet Sauvignon,'89, La Cuesta Vnyd., Res. (B-San Diego)
Chardonnay,'89, Santa Barbara Co. (B-San Diego)

CARMENET
1700 Moon Mountain Rd Sonoma 95476
Red Meritage,'88, Sonoma Vly., Estate (B-Orange)

CARNEROS CREEK WINERY
1285 Dealy Lane Napa 94559
Chardonnay,'90, Los Carneros $12.50 (2)
Pinot Noir,'89, Los Carneros $14.50 (3)
Pinot Noir,'90, Carneros, Fleur De Carneros $9.50 (B-Orange)

MAURICE CARRIE WINERY
34225 Rancho Calif. Rd. Temecula 92390
Cabernet Sauvignon,'90, Temecula $8.00 (2)
Chardonnay,'89, Temecula $7.50 (2)
Chenin Blanc,'90, Temecula, Estate, Soft $5.00 (3)
Johannisberg Riesling,'91, Temecula $5.00 (S-San Diego)
Pinot Noir,'90, Santa Barbara Co. $12.00 (B-Farmers)
Sauvignon Blanc,'90, Temecula, Estate $5.00 (B-Farmers)
White Zinfandel,'90, Temecula $5.00 (B-Dallas)

CASK ONE
Address not available
Cabernet Sauvignon,'88, Napa $7.00 (B-San Fran)
Chardonnay,'90, Mendocino (2)

CASTORO CELLARS
1480 No. Bethel Road Templeton 93465
Cabernet Sauvignon,'89, Paso Robles $10.00 (5)
Chardonnay,'90, San Luis Obispo Co. $9.50 (B-Dallas)
Chardonnay,'91, San Luis Obispo Co. $9.50 (4)
Pinot Noir,'89, Santa Barbara Co. $10.50 (B-Farmers)
White Zinfandel,'91, San Luis Obispo Co. $6.00 (6)
Zinfandel,'90, Paso Robles $9.00 (6)

CAVISTE
Address not available
Zinfandel,'90, Napa Vly. (B-Orange)

CAYMUS VINEYARDS
8700 Conn Creek Road Rutherford 94573
Cabernet Sauvignon,'89, Napa Vly. $24.00 (2)
Sauvignon Blanc,'91, Napa Vly. (B-State Fair)
Zinfandel,'89, Napa Vly. (2)
Zinfandel,'90, Napa Vly. (S-Orange)

CHALK HILL WINERY
10300 Chalk Hill Rd. Healdsburg 95448
Cabernet Sauvignon,'89, Chalk Hill, Estate $13.00 (2)
Chardonnay,'90, Sonoma Co., Chalk Hill, Estate $15.00 (8)
Sauvignon Blanc,'90, Sonoma Co., Chalk Hill $9.00 (B-W. Coast)

CHALONE VINEYARDS

P. O. Box 855 Soledad 93960

Chardonnay,'90, Chalone, Estate (B-Orange)

CHANDELLE OF SONOMA

14301 Arnold Drive Glen Ellen 95442

Chardonnay,'90, Sonoma Co., Chandelle Vnyd. $8.00 (2)

CHAPPELLET VINEYARD

1581 Sage Canyon Rd St Helena 94574

Chardonnay,'89, Napa Vly. $14.00 (2)
Chenin Blanc,'89, Napa Vly. $7.50 (3)
Merlot,'89, Napa Vly. $16.00 (3)

CHASE LIMOGERE

P. O. Box 55 Woodbridge 95258

Sparkling Wine,'NV, California, Brut $6.00 (3)

CHATEAU DE BAUN WINERY

5007 Fulton Road Fulton 95439

Chardonnay,'90, Russian River Vly., Barrel Ferm. $10.00 (8)
Pinot Noir,'90, California, Barrel Sel., Chateau Rouge $6.00 (2)
Sparkling Wine,'88, Sonoma Co., Rhapsody, Brut Rose $11.00 (3)
Sparkling Wine,'88, Sonoma Co., Romance, Brut $11.00 (3)

CHATEAU DE LEU WINERY

1635 W. Mason Rd Suisun 94585

Cabernet Sauvignon,'89, Napa Vly. $14.00 (5)
Chardonnay,'90, Solano Co., Green Vly. $14.00 (2)
Merlot,'90, Napa Vly. $12.00 (3)
Pinot Noir,'90, Napa Vly. $12.00 (5)
Sauvignon Blanc,'90, Napa Vly. $6.00 (3)

CHATEAU JULIEN WINERY

8940 Carmel Valley Rd. Carmel 93923

Cabernet Sauvignon,'89, Monterey Co. (B-W. Coast)
Cabernet Sauvignon,'89, Monterey Co., Res. $17.00 (B-Orange)
Chardonnay,'90, Monterey Co., Sur Lie, Reserve $15.00 (3)
Merlot,'89, Monterey Co. $14.00 (3)
White Meritage,'90, Monterey Co., Platinum $10.00 (2)

CHATEAU POMIJE WINERY

Address not available

Cabernet Sauvignon,'89, San Luis Obispo, Res. (B-San Diego)
Chardonnay,'NV, San Luis Obispo Co. (B-San Diego)

CHATEAU POTELLE

845 Oak Grove Ave., #115 Menlo Park 94025

Cabernet Sauvignon,'88, Alexander Vly. $16.00 (2)
Sauvignon Blanc,'91, Napa Vly. $8.95 (3)

CHATEAU SOUVERAIN

400 Souverain Road Geyserville 95441

Cabernet Sauvignon,'87, Alexander Vly., Res. $15.00 (G-San
Cabernet Sauvignon,'88, Alexander Vly. $10.00 (3)
Cabernet Sauvignon,'88, Alexander Vly., Reserve $15.00 (S-L.A.)
Cabernet Sauvignon,'89, Alexander Vly. $10.00 (B-San Fran)
Chardonnay,'88, Carneros, Reserve $14.00 (2)
Chardonnay,'90, Sonoma Co. $9.00 (S-State Fair)
Chardonnay,'90, Sonoma, Durrell Vnyd., Res. $14.00 (S-San Fran)

Merlot,'89, Alexander Vly. $10.00 (5)
Merlot,'90, Alexander Vly. (G-State Fair)
Merlot,'90, Sonoma Co. $10.00 (3)
Sauvignon Blanc,'90, Alexander Vly. $7.00 (B-W. Coast)
Zinfandel,'89, Dry Creek Vly. $7.50 (3)

CHATEAU ST. JEAN

8555 Sonoma Hwy. Kenwood 95452

Cabernet Sauvignon,'88, Sonoma Co. $18.00 (7)
Chardonnay,'89, Alexander Vly., Belle Terre $18.00 (2)
Chardonnay,'90, Alex. Vly., Robt Young $23.00 (B-San Diego)
Chardonnay,'90, Sonoma Co. (S-Orange)
Chardonnay,'90, Sonoma Vly., Estate Selection (2)
Gewurztraminer,'89, Russian River, Johnson Vnyd., SLH (S-Nat'l O.S.)
Gewurztraminer,'90, Alexander Vly., Belle Terre, SLH $15.00 (3)
Johannisberg Riesling,'91, Sonoma Co. (B-L.A.)
Sauvignon Blanc,'90, Russian River, La Petite Etoile $11.25
Sauvignon Blanc,'90, Sonoma Co., Fume $8.00 (B-Farmers)
Sparkling Wine,'82, Brut, Grande Cuvee (G-L.A.)
Sparkling Wine,'89, Sonoma Co. Blanc De Blanc (S-W. Coast)
Sparkling Wine,'89, Sonoma Co. Brut (B-W. Coast)
Sparkling Wine,'NV, Sonoma Co., Blanc De Blanc $12.00 (3)
Sparkling Wine,'NV, Sonoma Co., Brut $12.00 (3)

CHATEAU THOMAS

Address not available

Chardonnay,'88, Los Carneros, Sangiacomo (B-San Diego)

CHATOM VINEYARDS

7449 Esmeralda Rd San Andreas 95249

Cabernet Sauvignon,'89, Calaveras Co. $14.00 (4)
Chardonnay,'90, Calaveras Co. (B-San Diego)

CHAUFFE-EAU CELLARS

24401 Chianti Road Geyserville 95441

Cabernet Sauvignon,'87, Alexander Vly. $16.00 (5)
Chardonnay,'90, Carneros, Sangiacomo $16.00 (3)

CHERRYBLOCK

389 Fourth St. E. Sonoma 95476

Cabernet Sauvignon,'87, Sonoma Vly. (B-Orange)

CHESTNUT HILL

75 Broadway, #207 San Francisco 94111

Sauvignon Blanc,'90, North Coast $6.00 (S-Nat'l O.S.)
Sauvignon Blanc,'91, North Coast $6.00 (S-Orange)
Zinfandel,'89, San Luis Obispo Co. $6.00 (2)

CHEVAL SAUVAGE

P. O. Box 638 Templeton 93465

Merlot,'89, $25.00 (G-L.A.)
Merlot,'90, Paso Robles $25.00 (S-State Fair)
Pinot Noir,'89, Santa Barbara Co. $25.00 (G-State Fair)
Pinot Noir,'90, Paso Robles $25.00 (3)
Pinot Noir,'90, Santa Barbara Co. $25.00 (5)

CHIMNEY ROCK

5320 Silverado Trail Napa 94558

Cabernet Sauvignon,'87, Napa Vly., Stags Leap (S-Orange)

CHRISTIAN BROTHERS

P. O. Box 391 St Helena 94574

Cabernet Sauvignon,'88, Napa Vly. $7.50 (B-Nat'l O.S.)
White Zinfandel,'91, California $4.50 (2)

CHRISTOPHER CREEK

641 Limerick Lane Healdsburg 95448

Petite Sirah,'88, Russian River Vly. $11.00 (4)

CILURZO VINEYARD

41220 Calle Contento Temecula 92390

Cabernet Sauvignon,'86, Temecula (S-San Diego)
Merlot,'90, Temecula, Prop. Reserve (B-San Diego)
Petite Sirah,'85, Temecula, Estate (B-Nat'l O.S.)
Petite Sirah,'87, Temecula, Estate $12.00 (2)
Petite Sirah,'91, Temecula, Estate, Nouveau $7.00 (3)

CINNABAR

Address not available

Chardonnay,'89, Santa Cruz Mtns. Estate (S-Orange)

CLAIBORNE & CHURCHILL

860 Capitolio Way San Luis Obispo 93406

Gewurztraminer,'91, Central Coast, Alsatian Style (S-Orange)
Johannisberg Riesling,'91, Central Coast, Alsatian (B-Orange)

CLAIRVAUX

3291 Westside Rd. Healdsburg 95448

Merlot,'89, Napa Vly. $12.00 (2)

CLINE CELLARS

24737 Arnold Drive Sonoma 95476

Zinfandel,'90, Contra Costa Co. $9.00 (2)

CLONINGER CELLARS

Address not available

Chardonnay,'89, Monterey Co. (2)

CLOS DU BOIS

5 Fitch Street Healdsburg 95448

Cabernet Sauvignon,'88, Alexander Vly. $12.00 (G-Dallas)
Cabernet Sauvignon,'88, Alexander Vly., Briarcrest $21.00 (5)
Cabernet Sauvignon,'89, Alexander Vly. $13.00 (B-San Fran)
Chardonnay,'89, Dry Creek Vly. (S-W. Coast)
Chardonnay,'90, Alexander Vly. $12.00 (B-W. Coast)
Chardonnay,'90, Alexander Vly., Calcaire $18.50 (G-Orange)
Chardonnay,'90, Dry Creek Vly., Flintwood $17.00 (3)
Chardonnay,'91, Alexander Vly. $12.00 (2)
Gewurztraminer,'91, Alexander Vly. $8.00 (S-Orange)
Merlot,'89, Sonoma Co. $15.00 (4)
Red Meritage,'88, Alexander Vly., Marlstone $20.00 (4)
Red Meritage,'89, Alexander Vly., Marlstone $20.00 (3)
Sauvignon Blanc,'90, Alexander Vly. $8.00 (B-Nat'l O.S.)
Sauvignon Blanc,'91, Alexander Vly., Barrel Ferm. $8.00 (2)

CLOS DU MURIEL

40620 Calle Contento Temecula 92390

Chardonnay,'89, California $7.00 (2)
Sauvignon Blanc,'90, Temecula, Sur-Lie Re. $6.00 (G-Farmers)

CLOS DU VAL

5330 Silverado Trail Napa 94558

Merlot,'89, Napa, Stags Leap, Estate $20.00 (3)
Pinot Noir,'88, Napa Vly., Carneros $14.00 (2)
Zinfandel,'88, Napa Vly., Stags Leap Dist., Estate $14.00 (3)

CLOS PEGASE WINERY

1060 Dunaweal Ln. Calistoga 94515

Cabernet Sauvignon,'86, Napa Vly. $18.50 (2)
Cabernet Sauvignon,'87, Napa Vly. $18.50 (4)
Chardonnay,'88, Los Carneros $16.50 (3)
Chardonnay,'89, Napa Vly. $12.00 (2)
Chardonnay,'89, Sonoma Co., Hommage $20.00 (B-Farmers)
Merlot,'88, Napa Vly. $15.00 (2)
Sauvignon Blanc,'89, Napa Vly. $9.50 (4)

B. R. COHN

P.O. Box 1673 Sonoma 95476

Cabernet Sauvignon,'89, Napa Co., Silver Label (2)
Cabernet Sauvignon,'89, Sonoma Vly., Olive Hill Vnyd. $25.00 (3)
Merlot,'90, (B-L.A.)

CHRISTOPHER COLUMBUS

Address not available

Sauvignon Blanc,'NV, Central Coast $7.99 (B-Farmers)

CONCANNON VINEYARD

4590 Tesla Road Livermore 94550

Cabernet Sauvignon,'87, Livermore Vly., Estate $16.00 (B-San Fran)
Chardonnay,'88, Santa Clara Vly., Mistral Vnyd. $11.75 (3)
Petite Sirah,'85, Livermore Vly., Estate, Reserve $14.50 (4)

CONN CREEK WINERY

8711 Silverado Trail St Helena 94574

Cabernet Sauvignon,'87, Napa Vly. $17.00 (4)
Cabernet Sauvignon,'87, Napa Vly., Reserve $23.00 (6)
Merlot,'89, Napa Vly. $16.00 (3)
Red Meritage,'87, Napa Vly., Triomphe $26.00 (5)
Zinfandel,'87, Napa Vly. $10.00 (B-Nat'l O.S.)

COOKS CHAMPAGNE CELLARS

391 Taylor Blvd., #110 Pleasant Hill 94523

Chardonnay,'91, Cook's Captains Reserve (S-L.A.)
Merlot,'89, California (S-W. Coast)
Merlot,'90, California (B-State Fair)
Sparkling Wine,'NV, American Spumante $3.99 (4)
Sparkling Wine,'NV, American, Brut $3.99 (B-State Fair)
Sparkling Wine,'NV, American, Grand Re. $3.99 (B-State Fair)
Sparkling Wine,'NV, American, Imperial Blush $3.99 (3)
Sparkling Wine,'NV, American, Imperial Extra Dry $3.99 (2)
Sparkling Wine,'NV, American, Imperial White Zinfandel $3.99 (5)
White Zinfandel,'91, California $3.99 (B-W. Coast)

CORBETT CANYON VINEYARDS

2195 Corbett Canyon Rd. San Luis Obispo 93406

Cabernet Sauvignon,'89, Alexander Vly., Reserve $9.00 (2)
Cabernet Sauvignon,'89, California, Coastal Classic $8.00 (3)
Chardonnay,'91, Central Coast, Coastal Classic $8.00 (2)
Merlot,'89, California, Coastal Classic $8.00 (5)

Pinot Noir,'90, Santa Barbara Co., Reserve $9.00 (2)
Pinot Noir,'90, Santa Barbara, Coastal Classic $8.00 (S-Orange)
Sauvignon Blanc,'90, Paso Robles, Reserve (B-Orange)
Sauvignon Blanc,'91, Central Coast, Coastal Classic $6.00 (3)
White Zinfandel,'91, California, Coastal Classic $5.00 (3)

CORDONIU NAPA

1345 Henry Road Napa 94558

Sparkling Wine,'NV, Napa Vly, Brut (G-Orange)

CORISON

Address not available

Cabernet Sauvignon,'88, Napa Vly. (B-Orange)

COS

Address not available

Red Meritage,'89, Napa Vly. $45.00 (2)

COSENTINO WINERY

7415 St. Helena Hwy. Yountville 94599

Cabernet Sauvignon,'87, North Coast. Reserve $27.00 (2)
Cabernet Sauvignon,'88, North Coast, Reserve $27.00 (3)
Cabernet Sauvignon,'89, Napa Vly. $12.00 (B-San Fran)
Chardonnay,'90, Napa Vly., The Sculptor (2)
Merlot,'89, Napa Vly. $18.00 (3)
Pinot Noir,'90, Napa Co. (S-L.A.)
Pinot Noir,'90, Sonoma Co. (S-Orange)
Red Meritage,'88, California, The Poet $25.00 (B-Nat'l O.S.)
Red Meritage,'89, California, The Poet $25.00 (G-Farmers)

CRESTON VINEYARDS

679 Calf Canyon Hwy. Creston 93432

Cabernet Sauvignon,'87, Paso Robles, Winemakers Sel. $25.00 (4)
Cabernet Sauvignon,'88, Paso Robles (B-State Fair)
Chardonnay,'89, Paso Robles, Barrel Ferm. (2)
Merlot,'89, Paso Robles $15.00 (4)
Pinot Noir,'90, Paso Robles $9.00 (6)
White Meritage,'91, Paso Robles, Estate, Chevrier Blanc $9.00 (2)
White Zinfandel,'91, Paso Robles $6.00 (3)
Zinfandel,'90, Paso Robles, Estate $9.75 (4)

CRICHTON HALL

P. O. Box 9008 Rutherford 94573

Chardonnay,'90, Napa Vly., Chardonnay Vnyd. (2)

CULBERTSON WINERY

2608 Via Rancheros Fallbrook 92028

Sparkling Wine,'84, California (S-W. Coast)
Sparkling Wine,'84, California, Reserve (S-Nat'l O.S.)
Sparkling Wine,'86, California, Blanc De Blanc $20.00 (2)
Sparkling Wine,'87, California, Blanc De Noirs (G-W. Coast)
Sparkling Wine,'87, California, Brut (G-Nat'l O.S.)
Sparkling Wine,'87, California, Brut Rose (2)
Sparkling Wine,'87, California, Natural $16.00 (3)
Sparkling Wine,'NV, California Blanc De Noirs $12.00 (5)
Sparkling Wine,'NV, California, Brut $12.00 (5)
Sparkling Wine,'NV, California, Cuvee De Frontignan $16.00 (5)
Sparkling Wine,'NV, California, Cuvee Rouge $12.00 (5)

CUVAISON

P. O. Box 2230 Napa 94559

Cabernet Sauvignon,'88, Napa Vly. (B-Orange)

CYPRESS

1000 Lenzen Ave. San Jose 95126

Cabernet Sauvignon,'88, California $7.75 (3)
Chenin Blanc,'90, California, Dry (B-Orange)
Merlot,'89, California (S-Nat'l O.S.)
Sauvignon Blanc,'90, California, Fume (G-Orange)

D

DALLA VALLE VINEYARDS

7776 Silverado Trail Yountville 94599

Cabernet Sauvignon,'88, Napa Vly. (B-Orange)

DE LOACH VINEYARDS

1791 Olivet Rd. Santa Rosa 95401

Cabernet Sauvignon,'89, Russian River Vly., Estate $16.00 (5)
Chardonnay,'90, Russian River Vly. $15.00 (6)
Chardonnay,'90, Russian River Vly., O.F.S. $25.00 (2)
Gewurztraminer,'91, Russian River Vly., Estate $8.50 (4)
Gewurztraminer,'91, Russian River Vly., LH $14.00 (5)
Pinot Noir,'90, Russian River Vly., Estate (S-Orange)
Sauvignon Blanc,'90, Russian River Vly., Fume $9.50 (3)
Sauvignon Blanc,'91, Russian River Vly. $10.00 (3)
White Zinfandel,'91, Russian River Vly. $9.00 (7)
Zinfandel,'90, Russian River Vly., Estate $11.50 (7)
Zinfandel,'90, Russian River Vly., Estate, O.F.S. (B-Orange)

DE LORIMIER WINERY

P. O. Box 726 Geyserville 95441

Chardonnay,'90, Alexander Vly., Estate, Prism $15.00 (3)
Red Meritage,'87, Alexander Vly., Mosaic $18.00 (6)
White Meritage,'90, Alexander Vly., Spectrum $9.00 (3)

DE MOOR WINERY

P. O. Box 348 Oakville 94562

Chenin Blanc,'91, Napa Vly. $6.75 (3)
Sauvignon Blanc,'90, Napa Vly. (2)

DEER PARK WINERY

1000 Deer Park Rd. Deer Park 94576

Cabernet Sauvignon,'88, Beatty Ranch/Howell Mtn. Res. $24.00 (2)
Petite Sirah,'88, Napa Vly., Howell Mt. Park/Muscatine $14.00 (3)

DEER VALLEY VINEYARDS

P.O. Box 780 Gonzales 93926

Cabernet Sauvignon,'88, California $5.49 (3)
Chardonnay,'91, (S-L.A.)
Merlot,'90, California (2)
White Zinfandel,'91, California (2)

DEHLINGER WINERY

6300 Guerneville Rd. Sebastopol 95472

Cabernet Sauvignon,'88, Russian River Vly., Estate $15.00 (3)
Chardonnay,'90, Russian River Vly., Estate $13.00 (3)
Pinot Noir,'89, Russian River Vly., Estate $16.50 (5)

DELICATO VINEYARDS

12001 S. Hwy. 99 Manteca 95336

Cabernet Sauvignon,'89, Monterey (B-Orange)
Chardonnay,'91, Monterey (G-L.A.)
Chenin Blanc,'91, Monterey, Dry $4.25 (S-Orange)
Johannisberg Riesling,'89, Monterey, Ltd. Res. (B-San Diego)
Sauvignon Blanc,'89, Monterey $5.00 (2)
White Zinfandel,'91, California $4.25 (2)
Zinfandel,'89, Monterey (B-Orange)

DEUX AMIS WINERY

78670 Welter Lane Sebastopol 95472

Sauvignon Blanc,'90, Alexander Vly. (S-W. Coast)
Zinfandel,'90, Dry Creek Vly. (G-Orange)

DEVLIN WINE CELLARS

P. O. Box 728 Soquel 95073

Merlot,'89, Central Coast (B-San Diego)

DOMAINE BRETON

P. O. Box 1146 Middletown 95461

Chardonnay,'89, California $8.00 (2)
Chardonnay,'90, California $8.00 (2)
Sauvignon Blanc,'89, Lake Co. (S-San Diego)
Sauvignon Blanc,'90, North Coast $7.00 (3)
Zinfandel,'89, Lake Co. (B-Dallas)

DOMAINE CARNEROS

1240 Duhig Road Napa 94558

Sparkling Wine,'NV, Carneros, Brut $17.00 (2)

DOMAINE CHANDON

California Dr. Yountville 94599

Sparkling Wine,'NV, Napa Co., Brut Cuvee (S-Orange)
Sparkling Wine,'NV, Napa Vly., Reserve (S-Orange)
Sparkling Wine,'NV, Napa/Sonoma Co. Brut $13.50 (G-Farmers)
Sparkling Wine,'NV, Napa/Sonoma, Blanc De Noirs (G-Orange)

DOMAINE DE CLARCK

7023 Carmel Valley Rd. Carmel 93923

Chardonnay,'90, Monterey Co. (B-Orange)
Chardonnay,'90, Monterey Co., Reserve (2)
Pinot Noir,'89, Sonoma Co., Villages (S-Orange)
Pinot Noir,'90, Monterey Co., Reserve (B-Orange)
Pinot Noir,'90, Monterey Co., Villages (2)

DOMAINE MICHEL

4155 Wine Creek Rd. Healdsburg 95448

Cabernet Sauvignon,'87, Sonoma Co. $19.00 (B-Farmers)
Chardonnay,'89, Sonoma Co. $15.00 (3)

DOMAINE MONTREAUX

4101 Big Ranch Road Napa 94558

Sparkling Wine,'86, Napa Vly. Brut (2)

DOMAINE NAPA WINERY

1155 Mee Lane St Helena 94574

Chardonnay,'89, Napa Vly. $12.50 (2)
Merlot,'90, Napa Vly. $12.50 (2)
Sauvignon Blanc,'90, Napa Co. $10.00 (3)

Sauvignon Blanc,'91, Napa Vly. $10.00 (G-San Fran)

DOMAINE ST. GEORGE WINERY

1141 Grant Ave. Healdsburg 95448

Chardonnay,'91, California $8.00 (B-W. Coast)
Merlot,'89, Sonoma Co. $8.00 (2)
Sauvignon Blanc,'90, Alexander Vly., Fume, Reserve (2)

DONATONI WINERY

10604 So. La Cienega Inglewood 90304

Cabernet Sauvignon,'85, (S-L.A.)

J. PATRICK DORE WINES

330 Ignacio Blvd. #B-35 Novato 94949

Cabernet Sauvignon,'87, Calif., Ltd. Rel., Lot 102 $6.00 (S-Orange)
Cabernet Sauvignon,'89, California $6.00 (B-Farmers)
Sauvignon Blanc,'91, California, Floral Series $4.00 (S-San Fran)
White Zinfandel,'91, California, Floral Series $4.00 (3)

DOS SABAS

32580 Rancho Calif. Rd. Temecula 92390

Chardonnay,'90, Temecula (S-Orange)
White Zinfandel,'90, (B-L.A.)

DREYER SONOMA WINERY

Address not available

Chardonnay,'90, Carneros $15.00 (3)

DRY CREEK VINEYARD

3770 Lambert Bridge Healdsburg 95448

Cabernet Sauvignon,'89, Sonoma Co. $14.00 (B-Orange)
Chardonnay,'88, Sonoma Co., Reserve $20.00 (3)
Chardonnay,'90, Dry Creek Vly., Reserve $20.00 (2)
Chardonnay,'90, Sonoma Co. $13.25 (4)
Chenin Blanc,'91, California $7.00 (9)
Merlot,'89, Dry Creek Vly. $14.00 (6)
Merlot,'90, Dry Creek Vly. $14.00 (B-L.A.)
Red Meritage,'87, Dry Creek Vly. $24.00 (7)
Sauvignon Blanc,'90, Sonoma Co., Fume $9.25 (2)
Zinfandel,'89, Dry Creek Vly. $11.00 (2)
Zinfandel,'90, Dry Creek Vly. $11.00 (G-State Fair)

DUCKHORN

3027 Silverado Trail St Helena 94574

Merlot,'89, Napa Vly. $20.00 (B-Orange)
Merlot,'89, Napa Vly., Three Palms Vnyd. $25.00 (S-Orange)

DUNNEWOOD VINEYARDS

391 Taylor Blvd., #110 Pleasant Hill 94523

Chardonnay,'90, North Coast, Barrel Select (2)
Merlot,'88, California, Barrel Select (B-San Diego)
White Zinfandel,'91, California (B-W. Coast)

DURNEY VINEYARDS

P. O. Box 222016 Carmel 93922

Cabernet Sauvignon,'90, Carmel Vly., Durney Vnyd. $12.00 (3)
Chardonnay,'89, Carmel Vly., Estate $17.00 (S-San Fran)
Chenin Blanc,'91, Carmel Vly., Estate (B-Orange)

DUSINBERRE WINERY
Address not available
Sparkling Wine,'90, Napa Vly., Marston Vnyd. (2)

E

EAGLE RIDGE WINERY
111 Goodwin Avenue Penngrove 94951
Zinfandel,'89, Amador Co., Grand Pere Vnyd. $12.00 (3)
Zinfandel,'89, Amador Co., Grand Pere Vnyd., LH $9.50 (2)

EBERLE WINERY
128 Fairview Paso Robles 93446
Cabernet Sauvignon,'88, Paso Robles, Estate $15.00 (3)
Zinfandel,'89, Paso Robles $12.00 (2)
Zinfandel,'90, Paso Robles, Sauret Vnyd. $12.00 (3)

ELIZABETH VINEYARDS
8591 Colony Drive Redwood Valley 95470
Zinfandel,'90, Mendocino $10.00 (4)

ELLISTON VINEYARDS
463 Kilkare Road Sunol 94586
Chardonnay,'91, Central Coast, Sunol Vly. Vnyd. (G-State Fair)
White Meritage,'91, Sunol Vly. Vnyd., Triomphe $10.00 (2)

EMERALD BAY
P. O. Box 221775 Carmel 93923
Cabernet Sauvignon,'89, Calif., Prop. Reserve (S-Orange)
Chenin Blanc,'91, California, Prop. Reserve (2)

ESTANCIA VINEYARDS
1178 Galleron Rd. Rutherford 94573
Cabernet Sauvignon,'89, Alexander Vly. $9.00 (3)
Chardonnay,'90, Monterey $9.00 (4)
Chardonnay,'91, $9.00 (B-L.A.)
Red Meritage,'89, Alexander Vly. $14.00 (2)
Sauvignon Blanc,'90, Monterey $7.50 (G-Farmers)
Sauvignon Blanc,'91, Monterey $7.50 (2)
White Meritage,'90, Monterey, Estancia Estates $12.00 (2)

ESTRELLA RIVER
Shandon Star Rte. Paso Robles 93446
White Zinfandel,'91, California, Prop. Res. $5.00 (3)
Zinfandel,'89, California, Prop. Reserve $6.00 (B-Farmers)

EVEREST
Address not available
Cabernet Sauvignon,'87, Dry Creek Vly. $10.00 (B-Orange)

EYE OF THE SWAN CELLARS
389 Fourth St. E. Sonoma 94776
Cabernet Sauvignon,'89, California (S-Orange)
Cabernet Sauvignon,'NV, California (2)

F

FALCONER CELLARS
Address not available
Sparkling Wine,'84, Russian River Vly. (B-San Diego)

FALLBROOK

2608 Via Rancheros Fallbrook 92028

Chardonnay,'89, Calif., Culbertson Home Vnyd. (S-Nat'l O.S.)
Chardonnay,'90, California (B-Orange)

FAR NIENTE

Acacia Lane Oakville 94562

Chardonnay,'90, Napa Vly. (B-Orange)
Pinot Noir,'86, California (B-Orange)

GARY FARRELL WINES

P. O. Box 342 Forestville 95436

Cabernet Sauvignon,'89, Sonoma Co., Ladi's Vnyd. $18.00 (6)
Chardonnay,'90, Russian River Vly. $18.00 (3)
Merlot,'89, Sonoma Co., Ladi's Vnyd. $18.00 (2)
Pinot Noir,'90, Russian River Vly. $16.00 (4)
Pinot Noir,'90, Russian River Vly., Allen Vnyd. $28.00 (7)
Pinot Noir,'90, Santa Barbara Co., Bien Nacido Vnyd. $24.00 (3)
Zinfandel,'90, Russian River Vly., Collins Vnyd. $14.00 (4)

FELTON EMPIRE

379 Felton Empire Road Felton 95018

Chardonnay,'90, Monterey Co., Reserve (B-Orange)

FENESTRA WINERY

2954 Kilkare Road Sunol 94586

Cabernet Sauvignon,'88, Monterey, Smith & Hook Vnyd. $15.00 (2)
Cabernet Sauvignon,'89, Livermore Vly. $13.00 (2)
Chardonnay,'90, Livermore Vly. $12.50 (2)
Merlot,'89, Livermore Vly. $13.00 (2)
Sauvignon Blanc,'90, Livermore Vly. $8.00 (S-San Fran)
Zinfandel,'89, Livermore Vly. (2)

FERRARI-CARANO VINEYARD

8761 Dry Creek Road Healdsburg 95448

Cabernet Sauvignon,'89, Alexander Vly. (B-Orange)
Chardonnay,'90, Alexander Vly. $20.00 (B-Orange)
Merlot,'89, Sonoma Co. (B-Orange)
Sauvignon Blanc,'90, Sonoma Co., Fume (G-Nat'l O.S.)
Sauvignon Blanc,'91, Sonoma Co., Fume (S-Orange)

GLORIA FERRER

23555 Highway 121 Sonoma 95476

Sparkling Wine,'85, Carneros Cuvee, Brut $20.00 (2)
Sparkling Wine,'87, Carneros, Brut $17.00 (3)
Sparkling Wine,'NV, Sonoma Co. Brut $14.00 (5)

FETZER VINEYARDS

13325 So. Highway 101 Hopland 95449

Cabernet Sauvignon,'86, Sonoma Co., Reserve $24.00 (5)
Cabernet Sauvignon,'88, California, Barrel Select $11.00 (5)
Cabernet Sauvignon,'89, California, Valley Oaks $7.00 (5)
Chardonnay,'90, Mendocino Co. $20.00 (2)
Chardonnay,'90, Mendocino Co., Barrel Select $11.00 (2)
Chardonnay,'90, Mendocino, Reserve $19.00 (S-San Fran)
Chardonnay,'91, California, Sundial $7.00 (5)
Chenin Blanc,'90, Mendocino Co. $6.00 (4)
Gewurztraminer,'90, California $6.00 (S-Dallas)
Gewurztraminer,'91, California $6.00 (5)

Johannisberg Riesling,'90, California $6.00 (G-Nat'l O.S.)
Johannisberg Riesling,'91, California $6.00 (6)
Merlot,'90, California (B-W. Coast)
Sauvignon Blanc,'90, California, Barrel Select $9.00 (2)
Sauvignon Blanc,'90, California, Fume $6.00 (B-Nat'l O.S.)
Sauvignon Blanc,'91, California, Fume $7.00 (2)
White Zinfandel,'91, North Coast $6.75 (G-W. Coast)
Zinfandel,'89, California, Barrel Select $9.00 (6)

FIDDLEHEAD CELLARS

Address not available

Pinot Noir,'90, Santa Maria Vly. $25.00 (2)

FIELD STONE WINERY

10075 Highway 128 Healdsburg 95448

Sauvignon Blanc,'91, Sonoma Co., Prop. Blend (S-Orange)

FIELDBROOK VALLEY WINERY

4241 Fieldbrook Rd. Fieldbrook 95521

Chardonnay,'90, Mendocino Co., Barra Vnyd. (G-San Diego)
Chenin Blanc,'90, Napa Vly., Frediani Vnyd. (G-Orange)
Pinot Noir,'88, Napa Vly., Beard Vnyd. (S-San Diego)
Red Meritage,'90, California (S-State Fair)
Sauvignon Blanc,'91, Mendocino Co., Quillen Vnyd. (2)
Zinfandel,'91, Mendocino, Pacini Vnyd. $11.00 (2)

FILSINGER VINEYARDS

39050 DePortola Rd. Temecula 92390

Cabernet Sauvignon,'88, Temecula, Estate (B-Orange)
Johannisberg Riesling,'91, Temecula $6.00 (2)

FIRESTONE VINEYARD

Zaca Station Rd. Los Olivos 93441

Cabernet Sauvignon,'88, (B-L.A.)
Chardonnay,'90, Santa Ynez Vly., Barrel Ferm. $12.00 (3)
Chardonnay,'91, Santa Ynez Vly., Barrel Ferm. $12.00 (S-L.A.)
Gewurztraminer,'91, Santa Ynez Vly. (4)
Johannisberg Riesling,'90, Santa Ynez Vly. $7.50 (S-Dallas)
Johannisberg Riesling,'91, Santa Barbara Co. $9.00 (S-Orange)
Johannisberg Riesling,'91, Santa Barbara, SSLH (G-L.A.)
Johannisberg Riesling,'91, Santa Ynez Vly. $7.50 (3)
Merlot,'89, Santa Ynez Vly. $12.00 (2)
Merlot,'90, Santa Ynez Vly. $12.00 (2)
Sauvignon Blanc,'91, Santa Ynez Vly. (2)

FISHER VINEYARDS

6200 St. Helena Rd. Santa Rosa 95404

Cabernet Sauvignon,'89, Napa/Sonoma $18.00 (B-San Fran)
Chardonnay,'89, Sonoma Co., Coach Insignia $15.00 (4)

FLORA SPRINGS

1078 W. Zinfandel Lane St Helena 94574

Cabernet Sauvignon,'88, Reserve (S-L.A.)
Chardonnay,'90, Napa Vly., Barrel Ferm. $23.00 (G-Orange)
Red Meritage,'88, Napa Vly., Trilogy $33.00 (2)

FLOREAL

1078 W. Zinfandel Lane St Helena 94574

Cabernet Sauvignon,'89, Napa Vly. (S-Orange)
Chardonnay,'90, (B-L.A.)

Merlot,'89, Napa Co. (B-Nat'l O.S.)
Merlot,'90, Napa Vly. (2)

THOMAS FOGARTY WINERY

5937 Alpine Road Portola Valley 94025

Cabernet Sauvignon,'86, Napa Vly. $15.50 (3)
Chardonnay,'88, Santa Cruz Mtns. $18.00 (B-State Fair)
Chardonnay,'90, Monterey, Ventana Vnyd. $16.00 (B-State Fair)
Gewurztraminer,'85, Russian River Vly., Aged Dry (S-State Fair)
Gewurztraminer,'91, Monterey, Ventana Vnyds. $10.00 (7)
Pinot Noir,'89, Santa Cruz Mtn., Estate $16.00 (3)
Sparkling Wine,'89, Santa Cruz Mtns., Brut (2)

FOLIE A DEUX WINERY

3070 St. Helena Highway St Helena 94574

Cabernet Sauvignon,'88, Napa Vly. (B-San Diego)
Chardonnay,'90, Napa Vly. $16.50 (2)
Chenin Blanc,'90, Napa Vly. (B-San Diego)
Chenin Blanc,'91, Napa Vly. $8.00 (3)
Sparkling Wine,'89, Napa Vly., Fantasie $18.00 (3)

FOPPIANO VINEYARDS

12707 Old Redwood Hwy. Healdsburg 95448

Cabernet Sauvignon,'89, (B-L.A.)
Petite Sirah,'90, Sonoma Co. $10.00 (4)

FOREST LAKE VINEYARD

Address not available

Cabernet Sauvignon,'88, California $6.00 (B-Farmers)
Sauvignon Blanc,'89, California $5.00 (B-Farmers)
White Zinfandel,'90, California $5.00 (2)

FORMAN

Address not available

Cabernet Sauvignon,'89, Napa Vly., Estate (S-Orange)

FORTINO

4525 Hecker Pass Hwy. Gilroy 95020

Cabernet Sauvignon,'83, Calif., Barrel Select (B-Orange)

FOXEN

Address not available

Chardonnay,'90, Santa Maria Vly. (S-Orange)
Pinot Noir,'90, Santa Maria Vly. (G-Orange)

FRANCISCAN OAKVILLE ESTATE

1178 Galleron Rd. Rutherford 94573

Chardonnay,'90, Napa Vly. $12.00 (4)
Chardonnay,'90, Napa Vly., Cuvee Sauvage $24.00 (4)
Merlot,'89, Napa Vly. $15.00 (3)
Red Meritage,'88, Napa Vly., Red Table Wine $20.00 (6)
Zinfandel,'90, Napa Vly. $13.00 (5)

FRATELLI PERATA

Address not available

Cabernet Sauvignon,'89, Paso Robles $12.00 (S-San Fran)
Merlot,'89, Paso Robles, Estate (B-Dallas)
Merlot,'90, Paso Robles, Estate $13.00 (2)

FREEMARK ABBEY

3020 St. Helena Hwy., No. St Helena 94574

Cabernet Sauvignon,'86, Napa, Sycamore Vnyd. (B-Dallas)
Cabernet Sauvignon,'88, Napa Vly. $16.00 (3)
Chardonnay,'89, Napa Vly., Carpy Ranch $22.00 (B-San Diego)
Chardonnay,'90, Napa Vly., Carpy Ranch $22.00 (3)
Johannisberg Riesling,'91, Napa Vly. $8.50 (2)
Johannisberg Riesling,'91, Napa Vly., Edelwein, LH (S-San Diego)

FREY VINEYARDS

14000 Tomki Road Redwood Valley 95470

Zinfandel,'90, Mendocino (B-State Fair)

FRICK

303 Potrero St. #39 Santa Cruz 95060

Petite Sirah,'89, Dry Creek Vly. (B-Orange)

J. FRITZ WINERY

24691 Dutcher Creek Cloverdale 95425

Chardonnay,'90, Dry Creek Vly. $9.50 (S-Orange)
Chardonnay,'90, Russian River Vly. $12.50 (G-Dallas)
Sauvignon Blanc,'90, Dry Creek Vly. $8.00 (2)
Sauvignon Blanc,'91, Dry Creek Vly. $8.00 (2)
Zinfandel,'89, Dry Creek Vly. $10.00 (G-San Fran)

FROG'S LEAP

3358 St. Helena Hwy. St Helena 94574

Sauvignon Blanc,'91, Napa Vly. (B-Orange)

J. FURST

Address not available

Sauvignon Blanc,'91, California (2)

G

GABRIELLI WINERY

10950 West Road Redwood Valley 95470

Chardonnay,'90, Mendocino $16.00 (6)
White Meritage,'90, Mendocino, Ascenza $12.00 (6)

GAINEY VINEYARD

3950 E. Hwy. 246 Santa Ynez 93460

Cabernet Sauvignon,'89, Santa Ynez Vly. $13.00 (B-Orange)
Chardonnay,'90, Santa Barbara Co. $13.00 (4)
Johannisberg Riesling,'91, Santa Ynez Vly. $8.00 (5)
Sauvignon Blanc,'90, Santa Barbara Co. $9.00 (S-Nat'l O.S.)
Sauvignon Blanc,'90, Santa Ynez Vly. $15.00 (2)

E. & J. GALLO

P. O. Box 1130 Modesto 95353

Cabernet Sauvignon,'85, Northern Sonoma $8.00 (B-Farmers)
Cabernet Sauvignon,'NV, California $5.00 (3)
Sauvignon Blanc,'89, California, Reserve $5.00 (3)
White Zinfandel,'91, California $5.00 (4)

GAN EDEN

4950 Ross Road Sebastopol 95472

Sauvignon Blanc,'88, Sonoma Co., Fume (B-San Diego)

GARLAND RANCH

P. O. Box 221755 Carmel 93923

Cabernet Sauvignon,'88, California (S-Nat'l O.S.)
Chardonnay,'91, California $5.99 (B-Farmers)
Merlot,'86, California $5.00 (3)
Merlot,'89, California (B-L.A.)
White Zinfandel,'91, California (2)

GAVILAN

Address not available

Chardonnay,'90, Chalone, Estate (B-Orange)

DANIEL GEHRS

Address not available

Chenin Blanc,'91, Monterey Co., Le Cheniere (S-Orange)

GEYSER PEAK WINERY

22281 Chianti Rd. Geyserville 95441

Cabernet Sauvignon,'87, Alexander Vly., Est. Res. $15.00 (B-Dallas)
Cabernet Sauvignon,'89, Alexander Vly. $9.00 (7)
Cabernet Sauvignon,'89, Alexander Vly., Est. Res. $15.00 (4)
Chardonnay,'90, Alexander Vly., Estate Reserve $13.00 (B-Dallas)
Chardonnay,'90, Sonoma Co. $8.00 (4)
Chenin Blanc,'91, Alexander Vly., Soft $5.50 (5)
Gewurztraminer,'91, California, Soft $5.50 (3)
Johannisberg Riesling,'90, Mendocino Co., LH $13.00 (2)
Johannisberg Riesling,'91, California, Soft $5.50 (4)
Johannisberg Riesling,'91, Russian River Vly., SSLH $16.00 (2)
Merlot,'89, Alexander Vly. $10.00 (4)
Merlot,'90, Alexander Vly. $10.00 (2)
Petite Sirah,'89, Alexander Vly. $15.00 (3)
Pinot Noir,'90, Russian River Vly. $7.00 (B-Farmers)
Red Meritage,'87, Alexander Vly., Res. Alexandre $20.00 (7)
Sauvignon Blanc,'90, Sonoma Co. $6.50 (5)
Sauvignon Blanc,'91, Sonoma Co $7.00 (4)
White Meritage,'91, Alex. Vly., Chateau Alexandre $13.00 (3)
White Zinfandel,'91, California $5.00 (S-Nat'l O.S.)

GIRARD WINERY

7717 Silverado Trail Oakville 94562

Cabernet Sauvignon,'89, Napa Vly., Estate $16.00 (B-San Fran)
Chardonnay,'88, Napa Vly., Estate, Reserve $25.00 (B-Farmers)
Chardonnay,'89, Napa Vly., Reserve $28.00 (S-San Fran)
Chardonnay,'90, Napa Vly., Estate $16.00 (4)
Chenin Blanc,'90, Napa Vly. $6.50 (S-State Fair)

GLASS MOUNTAIN

Address not available

Cabernet Sauvignon,'89, Napa Vly. (B-State Fair)

GLEN ELLEN WINERY

1883 London Ranch Rd. Glen Ellen 95442

Cabernet Sauvignon,'89, California, Prop. Reserve $6.00 (3)
Chardonnay,'91, California, Prop. Reserve. $6.00 (2)
Merlot,'90, California, Prop. Reserve $6.00 (4)
Sauvignon Blanc,'91, California, Prop. Reserve $5.00 (3)
White Zinfandel,'91, California, Prop. Reserve $5.00 (5)

GOLD HILL VINEYARD

5660 Vineyard Lane   Coloma   95613

Chardonnay,'89, El Dorado Co. $10.00 (2)
Chenin Blanc,'90, El Dorado $7.00 (2)
Red Meritage,'89, El Dorado, Estate $16.00 (5)

GOLDEN CREEK VINEYARD

4480 Wallace Road   Santa Rosa   95404

Cabernet Sauvignon,'89, Sonoma Co. $12.00 (9)
Merlot,'89, Sonoma Co. $12.00 (5)
Merlot,'89, Sonoma Co., Reserve $15.00 (2)
Red Meritage,'89, Sonoma Co., Caberlot $12.00 (4)

GOOSECROSS CELLARS

1119 State Lane   Yountville   94599

Chardonnay,'89, Napa Vly. $8.99 (3)
Chardonnay,'89, Napa Vly., Estate $11.99 (5)

GRAND CRU VINEYARDS

1 Vintage Lane   Glen Ellen   95442

Cabernet Sauvignon,'88, Sonoma, Prem. Sel. $12.00 (5)
Chardonnay,'89, Carneros, Premium Selection $13.50 (3)
Chenin Blanc,'91, Clarksburg $7.00 (4)
Sauvignon Blanc,'90, Sonoma Co., Prem. Selection $9.50 (2)

GRANITE SPRINGS WINERY

6060 Granite Springs Road   Somerset   95684

Cabernet Sauvignon,'90, Sierra F'hills, Latchan $10.00 (B-San Fran)
Petite Sirah,'89, Granite Hill Vnyd. $9.50 (G-L.A.)
Zinfandel,'89, El Dorado, Higgins Vnyd. $12.00 (3)
Zinfandel,'89, El Dorado, Twin Rivers Vnyd.   (2)
Zinfandel,'90, El Dorado, Latcham Vnyd., Res. $10.00 (B-San Fran)

GRATHAM VINEYARDS

Address not available

Chardonnay,'90, Sonoma Co., Ashland Park   (B-San Diego)
White Zinfandel,'91, California, Lyness Creek   (B-San Diego)
Zinfandel,'89, Sonoma Co., Ashland Park, Reserve   (S-San Diego)

GREAT WESTERN

P. O. Box 780   Gonzales   93926

Sparkling Wine,'NV, California,Grand Cuvee $9.00 (B-Orange)

GREENWOOD RIDGE VINEYARDS

24555 Greenwood Rd.   Philo   95466

Cabernet Sauvignon,'88, Mendocino, Estate $12.00 (3)
Chardonnay,'90, Mendocino $16.00 (3)
Johannisberg Riesling,'89, Anderson Vly., White Riesling $8.50 (2)
Johannisberg Riesling,'90, Anderson Vly., LH $18.00 (S-Orange)
Johannisberg Riesling,'91, Anderson Vly. $8.50 (B-San Diego)
Merlot,'89, Anderson Vly., Estate $16.00 (6)
Pinot Noir,'90, Anderson Vly. $15.00 (5)
Sauvignon Blanc,'91, Anderson Vly. $8.50 (B-Orange)
Zinfandel,'90, Sonoma Co., Scherrer Vnyd. $12.50 (8)

GRGICH HILLS CELLAR

1829 St. Helena Hwy.   Rutherford   94573

Cabernet Sauvignon,'83, Napa Vly. $20.00 (B-Nat'l O.S.)
Cabernet Sauvignon,'86, Napa Vly. $20.00 (4)
Chardonnay,'89, Napa Vly. $22.00 (2)

Chardonnay,'90, Napa Vly. $22.00 (S-Orange)
Sauvignon Blanc,'90, Napa Vly., Fume $11.00 (B-Dallas)
Zinfandel,'88, Sonoma $12.00 (3)

ROTH VINEYARDS

750 Oakville Cross Oakville 94562

Chardonnay,'90, Napa Vly. $14.00 (2)

UENOC WINERY

21000 Butts Canyon Rd. Middletown 95461

Cabernet Sauvignon,'85, Guenoc Vly., Res. $18.00 (B-San Fran)
Cabernet Sauvignon,'86, Lake Co. $12.00 (2)
Cabernet Sauvignon,'87, Lake Co. $12.00 (2)
Cabernet Sauvignon,'87, Napa, Beckstoffer, Res. $24.00 (B-San
Cabernet Sauvignon,'88, Napa Vly. $24.00 (S-Dallas)
Cabernet Sauvignon,'89, Lake Co. $9.00 (2)
Cabernet Sauvignon,'89, Napa Vly., Beckstoffer, Res. $24.00 (4)
Chardonnay,'89, Guenoc Vly., Estate $14.00 (B-Nat'l O.S.)
Chardonnay,'89, Guenoc Vly., Magoon, Res. $23.00 (S-San Fran)
Chardonnay,'90, California $8.50 (2)
Chardonnay,'90, Guenoc Vly., Barrel Ferm. $14.00 (3)
Chardonnay,'90, Guenoc Vly., Magoon Vnyd.. Res. $23.00 (3)
Chardonnay,'91, North Coast $13.00 (S-San Diego)
Chenin Blanc,'90, California $6.00 (5)
Merlot,'87, Lake/Napa Co. $14.00 (B-Dallas)
Petite Sirah,'88, Guenoc Vly. $14.00 (6)
Petite Sirah,'89, North Coast $14.00 (7)
Red Meritage,'87, Lake Co./Napa Co., Langtry $35.00 (B-Farmers)
Red Meritage,'88, Napa Co./Lake Co., Langtry $35.00 (8)
Red Meritage,'89, Lake Co. $35.00 (2)
Sauvignon Blanc,'90, Guenoc Vly. $10.00 (S-State Fair)
Sauvignon Blanc,'91, North Coast $10.00 (S-San Diego)
White Meritage,'89, Guenoc Vly., Langtry $17.00 (B-Dallas)
White Meritage,'90, Guenoc Vly., Langtry $17.00 (9)
White Meritage,'91, Guenoc Vly., Langtry $17.00 (B-State Fair)
Zinfandel,'89, California $9.50 (4)
Zinfandel,'90, California $9.50 (S-State Fair)

UGLIELMO WINERY

1480 East Main Ave. Morgan Hill 95037

Cabernet Sauvignon,'86, Santa Clara, Reserve $10.00 (4)
Zinfandel,'88, Santa Clara Vly., Estate Reserve $8.00 (3)

UNDLACH-BUNDSCHU

3775 Thornberry Road Sonoma 95476

Cabernet Sauvignon,'88, Sonoma Vly., Rhinefarm Vnyds. $12.00 (2)
Cabernet Sauvignon,'89, Sonoma Co., Rhinefarm Vnyds. $15.00 (3)
Chardonnay,'90, Sonoma Vly., Estate $12.00 (3)
Gewurztraminer,'90, Sonoma Vly., Rhinefarm Vnyd. $7.50 (B-Dallas)
Gewurztraminer,'91, Sonoma Vly., Rhinefarm Vnyd. $7.50
Merlot,'89, Sonoma Vly., Rhinefarm Vnyd. $16.00 (6)
Pinot Noir,'90, Sonoma Co., Rhinefarm Vnyd. $14.00 (2)
Zinfandel,'90, Sonoma Vly., Rhinefarm Vnyd., Estate $10.00 (3)

JSTAVE NIEBAUM COLLECTION

P. O. Box 402 Rutherford 94573

Cabernet Sauvignon,'87, Napa Vly. (B-Nat'l O.S.)
Cabernet Sauvignon,'87, Napa Vly., Mast Vnyd. $14.00 (3)
Cabernet Sauvignon,'88, Napa Vly., Tench (2)

Cabernet Sauvignon,'89, Napa Vly., Reference $14.00 (2)
Chardonnay,'89, Carneros, Bayview Vnyd. $13.50 (3)
Chardonnay,'89, Napa Vly., Carneros, Laird Vnyd. $12.50 (2)
Chardonnay,'89, Napa Vly., Reference $11.00 (S-Nat'l O.S.)
Chardonnay,'90, Napa Vly., Reference $11.00 (B-San Fran)
Merlot,'89, Napa Vly., Reference (2)

H

HACIENDA WINERY

1000 Vineyard Lane Sonoma 95476

Cabernet Sauvignon,'86, Sonoma Co. $15.00 (3)
Chardonnay,'90, Sonoma Co., Claire De Lune $15.00 (B-Orange)
Chenin Blanc,'91, Clarksburg, Dry $6.50 (3)
Red Meritage,'88, Sonoma Co., Antares $28.00 (3)

HAGAFEN CELLARS

P. O. Box 3035 Napa 94558

Cabernet Sauvignon,'88, Napa Vly. $20.00 (B-State Fair)
Johannisberg Riesling,'91, Napa Vly. $9.00 (B-San Diego)

HAHN ESTATES

P. O. Drawer C Soledad 93960

Cabernet Sauvignon,'88, Monterey, Estate $9.00 (G-San Fran)
Chardonnay,'90, Monterey, Santa Lucia Highlands $9.00 (2)

HAMBRECHT VINEYARDS

Address not available

Cabernet Sauvignon,'89, Dry Creek Vly. (S-Orange)

HANDLEY CELLARS

P. O. Box 66 Philo 95466

Chardonnay,'89, Anderson Vly. $11.00 (3)
Chardonnay,'90, Anderson Vly. $11.00 (S-San Fran)
Chardonnay,'90, Dry Creek Vly. $14.50 (4)
Gewurztraminer,'91, Anderson Vly. $8.00 (5)
Johannisberg Riesling,'90, Anderson Vly., SLH (G-Orange)
Sauvignon Blanc,'90, Dry Creek Vly. $8.00 (4)
Sparkling Wine,'87, Anderson Vly., Brut $15.00 (6)
Sparkling Wine,'87, Anderson Vly., Brut Rose (B-San Diego)

HANNA WINERY

4345 Occidental Rd. Santa Rosa 95401

Cabernet Sauvignon,'88, Sonoma Co. $18.00 (6)
Cabernet Sauvignon,'90, Sonoma Co. $14.00 (S-Orange)
Chardonnay,'90, Sonoma Co. $14.00 (3)
Sauvignon Blanc,'90, Sonoma Co. $10.00 (S-Dallas)

HANZELL

18596 Lomita Avenue Sonoma 95476

Cabernet Sauvignon,'87, Sonoma Vly. (B-Orange)

HARMONY CELLARS

P. O. Box 2502 Harmony 93435

Cabernet Sauvignon,'89, Paso Robles $11.75 (3)
Chardonnay,'90, Paso Robles $10.75 (B-Farmers)
Chardonnay,'91, Paso Robles $10.75 (B-Orange)
Johannisberg Riesling,'91, Paso Robles $8.00 (4)
Pinot Noir,'90, Paso Robles $10.50 (G-Nat'l O.S.)
White Zinfandel,'91, Paso Robles $5.75 (2)

HARRISON

Address not available

Cabernet Sauvignon,'89, Napa Vly., Estate Grown (B-Orange)

HART WINERY

32580 Rancho Calif. Rd. Temecula 92390

Chardonnay,'90, Temecula $12.00 (2)

Merlot,'89, Temecula $15.00 (B-Farmers)

HAVENS WINE CELLARS

1441 Calistoga Avenue Napa 94558

Merlot,'89, Napa Vly. (S-Orange)

HAWK CREST

5766 Silverado Trail Napa 94558

Cabernet Sauvignon,'89, California, Hawk Crest $9.00 (S-Farmers)

HAYWOOD WINERY

18701 Gehricke Rd. Sonoma 95476

Cabernet Sauvignon,'88, Sonoma, Los Chamizal (B-San Diego)

Chardonnay,'89, Sonoma, Los Chamizal Vnyd. $14.00 (2)

Chardonnay,'90, California, Vintners Select $8.00 (3)

Sauvignon Blanc,'90, Sonoma Vly., Los Chamizal $10.00 (3)

Zinfandel,'90, Sonoma Vly., Los Chamizal Vnyd. $14.00 (6)

HESS COLLECTION

4140 Redwood Road Napa 94558

Cabernet Sauvignon,'88, Napa Vly. $17.00 (B-Orange)

Cabernet Sauvignon,'89, California $9.50 (G-Orange)

HIDDEN CELLARS

1500 Cunningham Rd. Ukiah 95482

Chardonnay,'90, Mendocino Co. $12.00 (5)

Chardonnay,'90, Mendocino Co., Reserve $16.00 (3)

Sauvignon Blanc,'90, Mendocino Co. (B-Dallas)

Sauvignon Blanc,'91, California $9.00 (B-San Fran)

Zinfandel,'89, Mendocino Co., Pacini Vnyd. $10.00 (4)

WILLIAM HILL WINERY

1775 Lincoln Ave. Napa 94558

Cabernet Sauvignon,'88, Napa Vly., Reserve $24.00 (B-San Diego)

Cabernet Sauvignon,'89, Napa, Silver Label $14.00 (S-Orange)

Chardonnay,'89, Napa Vly., Estate, Reserve $18.00 (B-Farmers)

Chardonnay,'90, Napa Vly., Estate Reserve $18.00 (B-Orange)

LOUIS HONIG CELLARS

850 Rutherford Road Rutherford 94573

Cabernet Sauvignon,'88, Napa Vly., Estate (S-Orange)

HOP KILN WINERY

6050 Westside Rd. Healdsburg 95448

Cabernet Sauvignon,'88, Alexander Vly. $13.00 (B-Orange)

Gewurztraminer,'90, Russian River Vly. $7.50 (B-San Diego)

Gewurztraminer,'91, Russian River, M. Griffin Vnyd. $7.50 (2)

Johannisberg Riesling,'91, Russian River, M. Griffin Vnyd. $8.00 (2)

Petite Sirah,'89, Russian River, M. Griffin Vnyd. $15.00 (S-Orange)

Zinfandel,'90, Sonoma Co. $12.00 (3)

Zinfandel,'90, Sonoma Co., Primativo $15.00 (B-State Fair)

HOPE FARMS WINERY

P. O. Box 3620 Paso Robles 93447

Cabernet Sauvignon,'88, Paso Robles (B-Orange)
Cabernet Sauvignon,'89, Paso Robles (2)
White Zinfandel,'91, Paso Robles (S-Orange)

HOUTZ VINEYARDS

2670 Ontiveros Road Los Olivos 93441

Sauvignon Blanc,'90, Santa Ynez Vly., Houtz Vnyd. (B-State Fair)

HOWELL MOUNTAIN VINEYARDS

300 Glass Mtn. Road St Helena 94574

Zinfandel,'88, Napa Vly. (2)

HUSCH VINEYARDS

4400 Highway 128 Philo 95466

Cabernet Sauvignon,'88, Mendocino, La Ribera Vnyd. $14.00 (3)
Cabernet Sauvignon,'88, Mendocino, North Field $18.00 (5)
Cabernet Sauvignon,'89, Mendocino, La Ribera $8.00 (4)
Chardonnay,'88, Anderson Vly. $18.00 (S-Nat'l O.S.)
Chardonnay,'89, Anderson Vly., Estate, Reserve $18.00 (2)
Chardonnay,'90, Mendocino, Estate $12.00 (6)
Chardonnay,'91, Mendocino $12.00 (B-San Fran)
Chenin Blanc,'90, Mendocino, La Ribera Vnyd. $7.50 (B-Dallas)
Gewurztraminer,'90, Anderson Vly., Estate $8.50 (3)
Gewurztraminer,'91, Anderson Vly., Estate $8.50 (4)
Pinot Noir,'89, Anderson Vly., Estate $14.00 (2)
Sauvignon Blanc,'90, Mendocino, La Ribera Vnyds. $8.50 (2)
Sauvignon Blanc,'91, Mendocino, La Ribera Vnyd. $8.50 (2)

I

IMAGERY SERIES

1883 London Ranch Rd. Glen Ellen 95442

Petite Sirah,'88, Arroyo Seco $16.00 (4)
Sparkling Wine,'89, Carneros, Blanc De Blanc $25.00 (B-San Fran)
Zinfandel,'90, Dry Creek Vly., LH $16.00 (3)

INDIAN SPRINGS VINEYARDS

Address not available

Cabernet Sauvignon,'87, Sierra Foothills $11.00 (S-Farmers)
Cabernet Sauvignon,'88, Sierra Foothills $11.00 (3)
Chardonnay,'91, Nevada Co., Sierra Foothills (B-Orange)
Merlot,'89, Sierra Foothills $10.50 (2)
Sauvignon Blanc,'91, Nevada Co. (B-San Diego)

INGLENOOK NAVALLE

1991 St. Helena Hwy. Rutherford 94573

Chenin Blanc,'NV, California (B-Orange)
White Zinfandel,'91, California (G-Orange)
White Zinfandel,'NV, California (G-Orange)

INGLENOOK-NAPA VALLEY

1991 St. Helena Hwy. Rutherford 94573

Cabernet Sauvignon,'85, Napa Vly., Cask Res. $17.00 (S-Nat'l O.S.)
Cabernet Sauvignon,'87, Napa Vly. $9.50 (S-State Fair)
Cabernet Sauvignon,'87, Napa Vly., Reserve Cask $17.00 (4)
Cabernet Sauvignon,'88, Napa Vly. $9.50 (4)
Merlot,'88, Napa Vly., Reserve $12.00 (4)

IRON HORSE VINEYARDS

9786 Ross Station Road Sebastopol 95472

Chardonnay,'90, Sonoma Co., Green Vly. (S-Orange)
Sparkling Wine,'87, Green Vly., Blanc De Blanc (S-Orange)
Sparkling Wine,'88, Sonoma Co., Green Vly., Brut (G-Orange)
Sparkling Wine,'89, Green Vly., Wedding Cuvee (S-Orange)

J

J

1474 Alexander Vly. Rd. Healdsburg 95448

Sparkling Wine,'88, Sonoma Co., Brut $22.00 (2)

THOMAS JAEGER WINERY

13455 San Pasqual Rd. Escondido 95025

Merlot,'87, Napa Vly., Inglewood Vnyd. $15.00 (3)
Merlot,'90, San Diego Co. (B-San Diego)
Sauvignon Blanc,'90, San Diego Co. $8.98 (2)

TOBIN JAMES

P. O. Box 2459 Paso Robles 93447

Cabernet Sauvignon,'89, Paso Robles, Private Stash $14.00 (2)
Cabernet Sauvignon,'90, Paso Robles, Private Stash $14.00 (3)
Pinot Noir,'90, Santa Barbara Co., Sunshine $15.00 (4)
Zinfandel,'89, Paso Robles, Inspiration $12.00 (2)
Zinfandel,'90, Paso Robles, Blue Moon Reserve $12.00 (3)

JANKRIS VINEYARD

Rt. 2, Box 40 Templeton 93465

Merlot,'90, Paso Robles (B-State Fair)
Pinot Noir,'89, Central Coast $8.75 (S-Farmers)
Zinfandel,'89, Paso Robles $8.75 (2)

JEKEL VINEYARDS

40155 Walnut Avenue Greenfield 93927

Chardonnay,'86, Arroyo Seco, Gravelstone Vnyd. (S-Orange)
Chardonnay,'88, Arroyo Seco, Gravelstone Vnyd. (B-Nat'l O.S.)
Chardonnay,'89, Arroyo Seco (B-W. Coast)
Chardonnay,'90, Arroyo Seco, Estate $11.95 (2)
Johannisberg Riesling,'90, Arroyo Seco, LH $12.00 (B-Farmers)
Johannisberg Riesling,'90, Monterey $7.00 (2)

JEPSON VINEYARDS

10400 So. Highway 101 Ukiah 95482

Chardonnay,'89, Mendocino $13.50 (S-Orange)
Sauvignon Blanc,'90, Mendocino (S-Orange)
Sparkling Wine,'86, Mendo., Blanc De Blanc $16.00 (S-Orange)

JORDAN VINEYARD

1474 Alexander Vly. Rd. Healdsburg 95448

Chardonnay,'89, Alexander Vly., Estate $19.00 (S-San Diego)

JOUILLIAN VINEYARD

Address not available

Sauvignon Blanc,'90, Carmel Vly. $6.00 (2)
Sauvignon Blanc,'91, Carmel Vly. $7.00 (S-San Fran)

JUSTIN VINEYARDS

11680 Chimney Rock Rd. Paso Robles 93446

Cabernet Sauvignon,'89, Paso Robles $18.00 (B-State Fair)
Red Meritage,'89, Paso Robles, Reserve $22.50 (B-L.A.)

KAUTZ VINEYARDS

5490 Bear Creek Road Lodi 95420

Merlot,'89, California, Angels Creek (B-San Diego)

ROBERT KEENAN WINERY

3660 Spring Mtn. Rd. St Helena 94574

Cabernet Sauvignon,'88, Napa Vly. (B-State Fair)
Chardonnay,'90, Napa Vly. (B-Dallas)
Merlot,'89, Napa Vly. (G-Orange)

KENDALL-JACKSON WINERY

640 Mathews Rd. Lakeport 95453

Cabernet Sauvignon,'87, Calif., Prop. Grand Reserve $22.50 (7)
Cabernet Sauvignon,'89, California, Vintner's Reserve $13.00 (5)
Chardonnay,'89, Calif., Prop. Grand Reserve $22.50 (B-Dallas)
Chardonnay,'90, California, Prop. Grand Reserve $22.50 (4)
Chardonnay,'90, California, Vintner's Reserve $13.00 (2)
Chardonnay,'90, Santa Maria Vly., Camelot Vnyd. (B-Dallas)
Chardonnay,'90, Sonoma Vly., Durell Vnyd. $16.00 (5)
Chardonnay,'91, California, Vintner's Reserve $13.00 (5)
Chenin Blanc,'91, California, Vintner's Reserve $9.00 (B-San Fran)
Gewurztraminer,'91, California, Vintner's Reserve $9.00 (7)
Johannisberg Riesling,'90, Lake Co., Vintner's Reserve $9.00 (3)
Johannisberg Riesling,'91, California, Vintner's Reserve $9.00 (3)
Merlot,'89, California, Vintner's Reserve $14.00 (3)
Pinot Noir,'89, California, Vintner's Reserve $13.00 (4)
Red Meritage,'87, Cardinale $65.00 (2)
Sauvignon Blanc,'90, Califonia, Vintner's Reserve $9.00 (4)
Zinfandel,'88, Anderson Vly., DuPratt Vnyd. $20.00 (2)
Zinfandel,'88, Mendocino, Ciapusci Vnyd. $20.00 (2)

KATHRYN KENNEDY WINERY

13180 Pierce Rd. Saratoga 95070

Cabernet Sauvignon,'88, Santa Cruz Mtns. (G-L.A.)
White Meritage,'90, California, Premium $17.00 (B-San Fran)

KENWOOD VINEYARDS

9592 Sonoma Highway Kenwood 94552

Cabernet Sauvignon,'88, Sonoma, Jack London $20.00 (S-Dallas)
Cabernet Sauvignon,'89, Sonoma Vly. $14.00 (S-W. Coast)
Cabernet Sauvignon,'89, Sonoma, Jack London Vnyd. $20.00 (5)
Chardonnay,'90, Sonoma Co. (B-W. Coast)
Chardonnay,'90, Sonoma Vly. (B-W. Coast)
Chenin Blanc,'91, California $7.00 (3)
Pinot Noir,'90, Sonoma Vly., Jack London Vnyd. $15.00 (3)
Sauvignon Blanc,'90, Sonoma Co. $10.00 (S-Nat'l O.S.)
Sauvignon Blanc,'91, Sonoma Co. $10.00 (2)
Zinfandel,'89, Sonoma Vly., Jack London Vnyd. $14.00 (2)
Zinfandel,'90, Sonoma Co., Jack London Vnyd. $14.00 (2)

J. KERR WINERY

Address not available

Chardonnay,'90, Santa Barbara Co. (G-Orange)

KONOCTI WINERY

4350 Thomas Dr. Kelseyville 95451

Cabernet Sauvignon,'89, Lake Co. $10.00 (S-W. Coast)

Chardonnay,'90, Lake Co. $10.00 (2)
Johannisberg Riesling,'89, Lake Co., White Riesling $7.50 (3)
Merlot,'89, Lake Co. $10.00 (2)
Sauvignon Blanc,'90, Lake Co. Fume $7.50 (5)
White Meritage,'89, Clear Lake, Estate $14.00 (5)

KONRAD ESTATE

3620 Road B Redwood Valley 95470

Johannisberg Riesling,'89, Mendocino Co. (G-W. Coast)
Red Meritage,'89, Mendocino, Melange A Trois (3)
Zinfandel,'89, Mendocino Co. (B-W. Coast)

KORBEL

13250 River Rd. Forestville 95446

Sparkling Wine,'NV, California, Brut Rose $10.50 (S-Orange)
Sparkling Wine,'NV, California, Natural $12.50 (S-Orange)
Sparkling Wine,'NV, Cuvee Chardonnay $12.50 (S-Orange)
Sparkling Wine,'NV, Cuvee Pinot Noir, Res. $12.50 (S-Orange)

HANS KORNELL

1091 Larkmead Lane St Helena 94574

Sparkling Wine,'87, Sonoma, Blanc De Noirs $14.75 (B-Dallas)

CHARLES KRUG WINERY

2800 Main Street St Helena 95474

Cabernet Sauvignon,'88, Napa Vly., Estate $12.00 (2)
Chenin Blanc,'91, Napa $7.00 (B-San Fran)
Johannisberg Riesling,'90, Napa Vly. $9.00 (G-Orange)
Pinot Noir,'89, Napa Vly., Carneros (B-Dallas)
Pinot Noir,'90, Napa Vly., Carneros (B-Orange)
Sauvignon Blanc,'90, Napa Vly., Estate $8.50 (B-Farmers)

KUNDE ESTATE WINERY

Address not available

Chardonnay,'90, Sonoma Vly., Estate Reserve (G-Orange)
Sauvignon Blanc,'90, Sonoma Vly. (S-W. Coast)

L

LA CREMA

971 Transport Way Petaluma 94953

Chardonnay,'89, California, Reserve (B-Orange)
Chardonnay,'90, California $12.00 (B-Orange)
Chardonnay,'90, California, Reserve (B-Dallas)
Pinot Noir,'89, California $12.00 (2)
Pinot Noir,'90, California, Reserve $19.00 (B-San Fran)

LA JOTA VINEYARD

1102 Las Posadas Rd. Angwin 94508

Cabernet Sauvignon,'88, Napa Vly., Howell Mtn. (B-Orange)

LA TOURNELLE

2999 Monterey Salinas Hwy. Monterey 93940

Chenin Blanc,'90, Monterey, Ventana Vnyd. $5.00 (5)

LA VIELLE MONTAGNE

3851 Spring Mtn. Road St Helena 94574

Cabernet Sauvignon,'88, Napa Vly., Estate (B-Orange)

LAKESPRING WINERY

2055 Hoffman Lane Napa 94558

Cabernet Sauvignon,'88, Napa Vly., Res. Sel. $14.00 (S-Orange)
Merlot,'88, Napa, Yountmill Vnyd. $14.00 (B-Nat'l O.S.)
Merlot,'89, Napa Vly. $14.00 (B-W. Coast)
Sauvignon Blanc,'91, Napa Vly., Yount Mill Vnyd. $8.50 (4)

LAKEWOOD VINEYARDS

640 Mathews Rd. Lakeport 95453

White Meritage,'90, California $15.00 (4)

LAMBERT BRIDGE

4085 W. Dry Creek Rd. Healdsburg 95448

Cabernet Sauvignon,'89, Sonoma Co. $16.00 (3)
Chardonnay,'90, Sonoma Co. $14.00 (3)
Merlot,'89, Dry Creek Vly. $14.00 (2)
Merlot,'89, Sonoma Co., Library Reserve (G-Orange)
Sauvignon Blanc,'90, Sonoma Co., Fume $10.00 (2)

LANDMARK VINEYARDS

101 Adobe Canyon Rd. Kenwood 95452

Chardonnay,'90, Alex. Vly., Damaris Vnyd., Res. $16.00 (2)
Chardonnay,'90, Sonoma Co. $12.00 (5)
Chardonnay,'90, Sonoma Vly., Two Williams (B-San Diego)

LANG WINES

Address not available

Zinfandel,'89, El Dorado, Twin Rivers Vnyd. (B-State Fair)

LASCAUX

Address not available

Cabernet Sauvignon,'89, Napa Vly. $16.00 (S-San Fran)

LATROBE CELLARS

4861 Memory Lane Shingle Springs 95682

Sauvignon Blanc,'89, El Dorado Co. $5.00 (S-Farmers)

LAUREL ESTATE

P. O. Box 548 Glen Ellen 95442

Sauvignon Blanc,'90, North Coast (S-Orange)

LAUREL GLEN

P. O. Box 548 Glen Ellen 95442

Cabernet Sauvignon,'89, Sonoma Mtn. (G-Orange)
Cabernet Sauvignon,'89, Sonoma, Counterpoint (S-Orange)

LAURIER

6342 Bystrum Road Ceres 95307

Chardonnay,'89, Sonoma Co. $15.00 (3)

LAVA CAP WINERY

2221 Fruitridge Rd. Placerville 95667

Cabernet Sauvignon,'87, El Dorado, Estate $10.00 (3)
Chardonnay,'90, El Dorado $10.00 (3)
Chardonnay,'90, El Dorado, Estate, Reserve $14.00 (6)
Sauvignon Blanc,'90, El Dorado, Estate, Fume $7.00 (3)
Zinfandel,'89, El Dorado, Estate $8.50 (2)

LAZY CREEK VINEYARDS

4610 Highway 128 Philo 95466

Gewurztraminer,'91, Anderson Vly., Estate (S-Orange)

Pinot Noir,'90, Anderson Vly., Estate (S-Orange)

LE DOMAINE

Address not available

Sparkling Wine,'NV, California, Brut (B-Orange)
Sparkling Wine,'NV, California, Extra Dry (G-Orange)

LEEWARD WINERY

2784 Johnson Dr. Ventura 93003

Cabernet Sauvignon,'88, Alexander Vly. $13.00 (3)
Chardonnay,'90, Central Coast $11.00 (3)
Chardonnay,'90, Edna Vly. $15.00 (2)
Chardonnay,'90, Monterey $14.00 (3)
Pinot Noir,'90, Santa Barbara Co. $16.00 (2)

LIBERTY SCHOOL

8700 Conn Creek Road Rutherford 94573

Cabernet Sauvignon,'NV, Calif., Vintner Select (S-Orange)

LIMERICK LANE

1023 Limerick Lane Healdsburg 95448

Sauvignon Blanc,'91, Russian River Vly. (B-Orange)
Zinfandel,'90, Russian River Vly. $10.00 (4)

LIMUR

Address not available

Chardonnay,'90, Napa Vly. (S-Orange)

LIVINGSTON

1895 Cabernet Lane St Helena 94574

Cabernet Sauvignon,'88, Napa, Moffett Vnyd. (S-Orange)

LOCKWOOD VINEYARD

1044 Harkins Road Salinas 93901

Cabernet Sauvignon,'90, Monterey, Est. $9.00 (S-Orange)
Cabernet Sauvignon,'90, Monterey, Partners Res. $16.00 (4)
Chardonnay,'89, Monterey Co., Estate $13.00 (2)
Chardonnay,'90, Monterey, Estate $7.50 (3)
Chardonnay,'90, Monterey, Partners Reserve $13.00 (5)
Johannisberg Riesling,'91, Monterey, Dry $8.00 (2)
Johannisberg Riesling,'91, Monterey, Lockwood Vnyd. Estate (4)
Johannisberg Riesling,'91, Monterey, SLH (2)
Merlot,'90, Monterey, Estate (2)
Sauvignon Blanc,'91, Monterey, Estate $7.00 (B-San Fran)

J. LOHR WINERY

1000 Lenzen Ave. San Jose 95126

Cabernet Sauvignon,'88, California (B-W. Coast)
Cabernet Sauvignon,'88, Paso Robles, Seven Oaks $12.00 (3)
Cabernet Sauvignon,'89, Paso Robles, Seven Oaks $12.25 (3)
Chardonnay,'90, Monterey Co., Riverstone $12.00 (B-San Diego)
Johannisberg Riesling,'90, Monterey, Bay Mist $7.25 (B-Farmers)

LOLONIS WINERY

2901 Road B Redwood Vly 95470

Cabernet Sauvignon,'89, Mendocino Co., Reserve $16.00 (2)
Chardonnay,'90, Mendocino Co. $12.00 (B-Farmers)
Chardonnay,'90, Mendocino Co., Reserve $19.00 (4)
Sauvignon Blanc,'90, Mendocino Co., Fume (2)
Zinfandel,'89, Mendocino Co., Lot 2, Reserve $10.00 (2)
Zinfandel,'90, Mendocino Co. (S-State Fair)

Zinfandel,'90, Mendocino Co., Reserve $12.00 (4)

LONGORIA FAMILY WINES

2670 Ontiveros Road Los Olivos 93441

Merlot,'90, Santa Ynez Vly. $16.00 (2)

LYETH

24625 Chianti Road Geyserville 95441

White Meritage,'89, Alexander Vly. $22.50 (B-Orange)

LYTTON SPRINGS WINERY

650 Lytton Springs Rd. Healdsburg 95448

Zinfandel,'89, Sonoma Co. $15.00 (4)

M

MAACAMA CREEK

15001 Chalk Hill Rd. Healdsburg 95448

Cabernet Sauvignon,'89, Sonoma Co., Melim Vnyd. $9.00 (3)

MACROSTIE WINERY

17246 Woodland Ave. Sonoma 95476

Chardonnay,'90, Carneros $14.75 (B-San Diego)

MADDALENA VINEYARD

737 Lamar Street Los Angeles 90031

Cabernet Sauvignon,'88, Sonoma Co. $8.00 (2)
Chardonnay,'90, Central Coast $8.00 (2)

MADRONA VINEYARDS

P. O. Box 454, Gatlin Rd. Camino 95709

Cabernet Sauvignon,'85, El Dorado, Madrona Vnyd $12.00 (3)
Chardonnay,'89, El Dorado, Madrona Vnyd (S-Nat'l O.S.)
Johannisberg Riesling,'89, El Dorado $6.75 (B-Farmers)
White Zinfandel,'91, El Dorado $5.00 (G-Orange)
Zinfandel,'88, California, Madrona Vnyd. Estate, LH (B-Nat'l O.S.)
Zinfandel,'89, El Dorado, Madrona Vnyd. $8.50 (2)

MAISON DEUTZ WINERY

453 Deutz Dr. Arroyo Grande 93420

Sparkling Wine,'87, San Luis Obispo Co.,Brut Reserve $22.00 (5)
Sparkling Wine,'NV, SLO/Santa Barbara Brut Rose $24.00 (6)
Sparkling Wine,'NV, SLO/Santa Barbara Co., Brut Cuvee $15.00 (4)

M. MARION

5350 Skylane Blvd. #201 Santa Rosa 95403

Cabernet Sauvignon,'89, California (3)

MARK WEST VINEYARDS

7000 Trenton-Healdsburg Rd. Forestville 95436

Chardonnay,'90, Russian River Vly., La Beau Vnyd. $12.50 (2)
Gewurztraminer,'89, Russian River Vly. (B-Dallas)
Gewurztraminer,'91, Creekside Vnyd., Estate, LH $13.00 (3)
Pinot Noir,'90, Russian River Vly., Ellis Vnyd., Re. $22.00 (B-Farmers)
Sparkling Wine,'86, Russian River Vly. Blanc De Noirs $17.00 (2)
Zinfandel,'89, Sonoma Co., Robert Rue Vnyd. $17.00 (6)

MARKHAM VINEYARDS

2812 N. St. Helena Hwy. St Helena 94574

Cabernet Sauvignon,'88, $14.00 (S-L.A.)
Sauvignon Blanc,'91, Napa Vly. $8.00 (3)
Merlot,'89, (S-L.A.)

MARTINELLI VINEYARDS

3360 River Road Windsor 95436

Chardonnay,'90, Russian River Vly., Estate $10.00 (2)
Gewurztraminer,'91, Russian River Vly., Estate (2)

LOUIS M. MARTINI WINERY

254 St. Helena Hwy., N. St Helena 94574

Cabernet Sauvignon,'88, Napa Vly., Reserve $14.00 (G-San Diego)
Cabernet Sauvignon,'88, Sonoma, M. Rosso $12.00 (B-San Diego)
Cabernet Sauvignon,'89, California (B-Nat'l O.S.)
Chardonnay,'90, Las Amigas, Vnyd. Selection (S-Orange)
Chardonnay,'90, Napa Vly., Reserve $14.99 (S-Farmers)
Chardonnay,'90, Sonoma Co./Napa Co. $8.00 (2)
Merlot,'88, Russian River, Los Venedos, Del Rio (G-San Diego)
Merlot,'89, North Coast $8.00 (B-W. Coast)
Petite Sirah,'87, Napa Vly., Reserve $14.00 (6)
Pinot Noir,'88, Napa Vly., Carneros, La Loma Vnyd. $13.99 (2)
Pinot Noir,'90, (B-L.A.)
Sauvignon Blanc,'90, Napa Vly. $7.00 (4)
Zinfandel,'88, Sonoma/Napa Co. $8.00 (2)

PAUL MASSON VINEYARDS

13150 Saratoga Ave. Saratoga 95070

Cabernet Sauvignon,'88, Monterey Co. $7.99 (2)
Cabernet Sauvignon,'89, Calif., Premium, Vintners $5.00
Chardonnay,'90, Monterey Co. $7.50 (B-Dallas)
Merlot,'88, Monterey Co. $8.00 (2)
Merlot,'89, Monterey Co., Vintage Selection $8.00 (B-Orange)
Merlot,'90, Calif., Premium, Vintners Sel. $5.50 (B-Orange)
Pinot Noir,'88, Monterey Co., Vintage Selection (B-San Diego)
Sparkling Wine,'NV, Califonia, Brut (S-Orange)
Sparkling Wine,'NV, California, Extra Dry (B-Orange)
White Zinfandel,'91, Calif., Premium, Vintners Sel. (G-Orange)

MATANZAS CREEK WINERY

6097 Bennett Vly. Rd. Santa Rosa 95404

Chardonnay,'89, Sonoma Vly. $19.00 (S-Dallas)
Chardonnay,'90, Sonoma Vly. $19.00 (2)
Sauvignon Blanc,'90, Sonoma Co. (2)

ANTHONY D. MATERA WINE CELLARS

4300 Silverado Trail Napa 94558

Red Meritage,'NV, Napa Vly., Medley $10.72 (3)

MAYACAMAS VINEYARDS

1155 Lokoya Rd. Napa 94558

Cabernet Sauvignon,'80, Napa Vly (B-State Fair)
Sauvignon Blanc,'86, Napa Vly. (B-State Fair)

MAZZOCCO VINEYARDS

1400 Lytton Springs Rd. Healdsburg 95448

Cabernet Sauvignon,'88, Alexander Vly., Claret Style (S-Orange)
Chardonnay,'89, Alexander Vly. $16.00 (3)

MC DOWELL VALLEY VINEYARDS

3811 Highway 175 Hopland 95449

Sauvignon Blanc,'90, Mendocino $7.00 (B-San Fran)

MC HENRY VINEYARD
330 11th Street Davis 95616
Pinot Noir,'88, Santa Cruz Mtns. $12.50 (2)

MC ILROY WINES
Address not available
Chardonnay,'90, Russian River Vly. $15.50 (5)

MEEKER VINEYARD
9711 W. Dry Creek Rd. Healdsburg 95448
Cabernet Sauvignon,'86, Dry Creek Vly. $14.00 (2)
Cabernet Sauvignon,'87, Dry Creek Vly. $14.00 (2)
Cabernet Sauvignon,'88, Dry Creek Vly. $14.00 (S-L.A.)
Zinfandel,'89, Dry Creek Vly., Estate $10.00 (2)
Zinfandel,'89, Dry Creek Vly., Gold Leaf Res. (G-Dallas)

MELIM VINEYARDS
15001 Chalk Hill Rd. Healdsburg 95448
Cabernet Sauvignon,'89, Alex. Vly., Maacama Creek $12.00 (2)

MENDOCINO ESTATE
Address not available
Chardonnay,'91, Mendocino (B-W. Coast)

MENDOCINO HILLS VINEYARDS
Address not available
Cabernet Sauvignon,'89, Mendocino Co. (2)

MERIDIAN VINEYARDS
7000 Hwy. 46 East Paso Robles 93447
Cabernet Sauvignon,'89, Paso Robles $12.00 (6)
Chardonnay,'90, Edna Vly. $15.00 (3)
Chardonnay,'90, Santa Barbara Co. $10.00 (3)
Pinot Noir,'90, Santa Barbara Co. $14.00 (2)

MERLION
1216C Church Street St Helena 94574
Cabernet Sauvignon,'87, Napa Vly. $11.00 (S-Orange)

MERRY VINTNERS
3339 Hartman Rd. Santa Rosa 95401
Chardonnay,'89, Sonoma Co., Reserve $12.00 (S-San Diego)

MERRYVALE VINEYARDS
3640 Buchanan St. San Francisco 94123
Cabernet Sauvignon,'87, Napa Vly., Profile (B-Dallas)
Chardonnay,'90, Napa Vly., Starmont (2)
White Meritage,'91, Napa Vly. $12.00 (2)

MIETZ CELLARS
602 Limerick Lane Healdsburg 95448
Merlot,'90, Sonoma Co. $13.00 (B-San Diego)

MILAT VINEYARDS
1091 S. St. Helena Hwy. St Helena 94574
Chardonnay,'90, Napa Vly., Estate $10.00 (B-Farmers)
Chenin Blanc,'91, Napa Vly. Estate $6.95 (3)
White Zinfandel,'91, Napa Vly., Estate $6.25 (3)

MILL CREEK VINEYARDS
1401 Westside Rd. Healdsburg 95448
Gewurztraminer,'91, Dry Creek Vly. (2)

Merlot,'87, Dry Creek Vly. $10.00 (G-Dallas)
Merlot,'88, Dry Creek Vly. $10.00 (G-W. Coast)

MILLAIRE WINERY

276 Main Street Murphys 95247

Zinfandel,'90, Sierra Foothills, Eschen Vnyd. (B-State Fair)
Zinfandel,'90, Sierra Foothills, LH (G-State Fair)
Zinfandel,'90, Sierra Foothills, T.C. Vnyd. Selections (B-Orange)

MIRASSOU VINEYARDS

3000 Aborn Rd. San Jose 95135

Cabernet Sauvignon,'87, Monterey Co., Fifth Gen. (B-Orange)
Chardonnay,'90, Monterey Co., Family Selection $9.75 (2)
Chardonnay,'90, Monterey, 5th Gen., Harvest Res. $12.50 (6)
Chenin Blanc,'90, Monterey Co., Family Sel. $6.50 (B-Farmers)
Johannisberg Riesling,'91, (S-San Fran)
Petite Sirah,'89, Monterey Co., Family Selection $7.50 (3)
Pinot Noir,'88, Monterey Co., Ltd., Harvest Res. (S-San Diego)
Pinot Noir,'90, Monterey Co.,5th Gen. Family Sel. $7.50 (3)
Sauvignon Blanc,'90, California (B-Orange)
Sparkling Wine,'84, Monterey, 5th Gen. Cuvee Brul, Res. $15.00 (3)
Sparkling Wine,'85, Monterey, 5th Gen. Cuvee, Res. $15.00 (B-L.A.)
Sparkling Wine,'87, Monterey, Brut Reserve $15.00 (B-Nat'l O.S.)
Sparkling Wine,'88, Monterey, 5th Generation Cuvee, Brut (2)
Sparkling Wine,'88, Monterey,au Naturel, 5th Gen. Cuvee $15.00 (5)
Sparkling Wine,'89, 5th Gen. Cuvee Blanc De Noirs $12.00 (8)
White Zinfandel,'91, California $5.50 (2)
Zinfandel,'88, Santa Clara Vly. (B-State Fair)
Zinfandel,'NV, California, Lot 6 $5.50 (3)

MISSION VIEW ESTATE

P. O. Box 129 San Miguel 93451

Cabernet Sauvignon,'88, Paso Robles $12.00 (B-State Fair)
Zinfandel,'88, Paso Robles (S-Orange)

MOCERI CELLARS

1724 Laurel Street San Carlos 94070

Cabernet Sauvignon,'89, Sonoma Co. (2)
Cabernet Sauvignon,'89, Sonoma Co., Lot II (S-Orange)
White Zinfandel,'91, Amador Co. (G-Orange)

C. K. MONDAVI

2800 Main St. St Helena 94574

Cabernet Sauvignon,'NV, California (B-Orange)
Chardonnay,'91, California (B-Orange)
Chenin Blanc,'NV, California (S-Orange)

ROBERT MONDAVI WINERY

7801 St. Helena Hwy. Oakville 94562

Cabernet Sauvignon,'88, Napa Vly. $18.00 (2)
Cabernet Sauvignon,'88, Napa Vly., Unfiltered, Reserve $40.00 (3)
Chardonnay,'90, Napa Vly. $12.00 (B-San Diego)
Chardonnay,'90, Napa Vly., Reserve $26.00 (4)
Pinot Noir,'90, Napa Vly. $14.00 (3)
Pinot Noir,'90, Napa Vly., Unfiltered, Reserve $28.00 (2)

MONT ST. JOHN CELLARS

5400 Old Sonoma Rd. Napa 94558

Cabernet Sauvignon,'87, Napa Vly. $14.00 (B-Nat'l O.S.)
Chardonnay,'89, Napa Vly., Carneros, Estate (S-Nat'l O.S.)

MONTEREY PENINSULA WINERY
467 Shasta Ave. Sand City 93955
Cabernet Sauvignon,'85, Monterey Co., Reserve $25.00
Cabernet Sauvignon,'86, Monterey Cellars (G-L.A.)

MONTEREY VINEYARD
800 So. Alta St. Gonzales 93926
Cabernet Sauvignon,'89, Monterey, Classic $11.00 (B-L.A.)
Chardonnay,'90, Monterey Co., Classic (B-San Diego)
Merlot,'89, Monterey Co., Classic Merlot (B-Dallas)
Merlot,'90, Monterey Co., Classic Merlot (B-Orange)
Pinot Noir,'89, Monterey Co., Ltd. Release $8.00 (3)

MONTEVINA WINES
20680 Shenandoah School Plymouth 95669
Sauvignon Blanc,'91, California, Fume $6.50 (3)
White Zinfandel,'91, Amador Co. (G-Orange)
Zinfandel,'89, Amador Co. $9.00 (2)
Zinfandel,'89, Amador Co., Reserve (B-Orange)
Zinfandel,'90, Amador Co., Brioso (S-Orange)

MONTICELLO CELLARS
4242 Big Ranch Rd. Napa 94558
Cabernet Sauvignon,'88, Napa Vly., Jefferson Cuvee $15.00 (2)
Cabernet Sauvignon,'89, Napa Vly., Corley Reserve $25.00 (2)
Cabernet Sauvignon,'89, Napa Vly., Jefferson Cuvee $15.00 (2)
Chardonnay,'89, Napa Vly., Corley Reserve $17.25 (B-Farmers)
Chardonnay,'90, Napa Vly., Corley Reserve $17.25 (B-Orange)
Chardonnay,'90, Napa Vly., Jefferson Cuvee (B-Orange)

MONTPELLIER VINEYARDS
P. O. Box 789 Ceres 95307
Cabernet Sauvignon,'88, California $7.00 (B-State Fair)
Sauvignon Blanc,'89, California $6.00 (B-Orange)
White Zinfandel,'91, California $6.00 (4)

MORGAN
526-E Brunken Avenue Salinas 93901
Cabernet Sauvignon,'89, Carmel Vly. $18.00 (B-Orange)
Chardonnay,'90, Monterey (2)
Pinot Noir,'90, California $14.00 (2)
Sauvignon Blanc,'90, Sonoma Co. $9.00 (B-Dallas)

J. W. MORRIS WINERY
101 Grant Ave. Healdsburg 95448
Cabernet Sauvignon,'89, California, Private Reserve $8.00 (2)
Sauvignon Blanc,'89, California, Reserve $6.50 (2)
White Zinfandel,'91, California, Res. $5.00 (S-Farmers)

MOUNT EDEN VINEYARDS
22020 Mt. Eden Road Saratoga 95070
Cabernet Sauvignon,'89, Santa Cruz, Lathweissen (G-Orange)

MOUNT PALOMAR WINERY
33820 Rancho Calif. Rd. Temecula 92390
Chardonnay,'91, Temecula $10.00 (2)
Chardonnay,'91, Temecula, Reserve $16.00 (2)
Johannisberg Riesling,'91, Temecula $6.00 (5)
Sauvignon Blanc,'91, Temecula $8.00 (3)
Sauvignon Blanc,'91, Temecula, Reserve $12.00 (B-Orange)

White Zinfandel,'91, Temecula (2)

MOUNT VEEDER WINERY

1999 Mt. Veeder Rd. Napa 94558

Chardonnay,'90, Napa Vly. $17.00 (B-W. Coast)

Red Meritage,'88, Napa Vly., Red Table Wine $24.00 (7)

MUMM NAPA VALLEY

1111 Dunaweal Ln. Calistoga 94515

Sparkling Wine,'87, Cuvee Napa, Vintage Res. Brut $22.00 (3)

Sparkling Wine,'88, Winery Lake, Cuvee Napa, Brut $22.00 (3)

Sparkling Wine,'NV, Cuvee Napa, Brut Prestige $15.00 (6)

Sparkling Wine,'NV, Napa, Cuvee Napa Blanc De Noirs $15.00 (7)

MURPHY-GOODE WINERY

3740 Hwy. 128 Geyserville 95441

Cabernet Sauvignon,'88, Alexander Vly. $16.00 (2)

Cabernet Sauvignon,'89, Alexander Vly., Murphy Ranch $16.00 (2)

Chardonnay,'90, Alexander Vly. $11.00 (S-W. Coast)

N

NALLE

P. O. Box 454, Gatlin Rd. Healdsburg 95448

Cabernet Sauvignon,'88, Dry Creek Vly. (B-Orange)

NAPA CREEK

1001 Silverado Trail St Helena 94574

Chardonnay,'89, Napa Vly. $15.00 (2)

Chardonnay,'90, Napa Vly. $15.00 (2)

Merlot,'89, Napa Vly. (2)

NAPA RIDGE

P. O. Box 111 St Helena 94574

Cabernet Sauvignon,'89, North Coast $7.50 (3)

Cabernet Sauvignon,'89, Paso Robles $14.00 (B-San Fran)

Gewurztraminer,'90, Central Coast $5.50 (6)

Pinot Noir,'90, North Coast $6.00 (2)

Sauvignon Blanc,'90, North Coast $6.00 (B-Orange)

White Zinfandel,'91, Lodi $5.00 (B-Nat'l O.S.)

Zinfandel,'89, Central Coast $5.00 (B-Nat'l O.S.)

NAVARRO VINEYARDS

5601 Highway 128 Philo 95466

Cabernet Sauvignon,'87, Mendocino $16.00 (5)

Chardonnay,'89, Mendocino, Reserve $14.00 (B-Farmers)

Chardonnay,'90, Anderson Vly., Reserve $14.00 (4)

Chardonnay,'90, Mendocino $11.00 (B-State Fair)

Gewurztraminer,'89, Anderson Vly., CSLH $30.00 (G-Orange)

Gewurztraminer,'90, Anderson Vly. (dry) $8.50 (3)

Johannisberg Riesling,'90, Mendocino, CSLH $25.00 (3)

Johannisberg Riesling,'90, Mendocino, LH $12.00 (5)

Johannisberg Riesling,'91, Mendocino $9.00 (2)

Pinot Noir,'88, Anderson Vly., Methode A L'Ancienne $14.00 (2)

Pinot Noir,'89, Anderson Vly., Methode L'Ancienne $14.00 (2)

Pinot Noir,'89, Mendocino, Table Wine $8.00 (2)

Sauvignon Blanc,'90, Mendocino $9.75 (2)

NEVADA CITY WINERY

321 Spring St. Nevada City 95959

Cabernet Sauvignon,'89, Nevada Co., Sierra Foothill $11.00 (3)
Merlot,'89, Nevada Co., Sierra Foothill $13.00 (3)
Red Meritage,'89, Sierra Foothills, Dir. Reserve $14.00 (5)
Zinfandel,'90, Sierra Foothills $6.00 (2)

NEVADA COUNTY WINE GUILD

Address not available

Pinot Noir,'90, Nevada Co. (B-Orange)
Zinfandel,'90, Nevada Co. (B-Orange)

NEWLAN VINEYARDS

1305 Carrell Lane Napa 94558

Cabernet Sauvignon,'86, Napa, Estate $15.00 (B-San Fran)
Pinot Noir,'89, Napa Vly. $18.00 (2)

NEWTON VINEYARD

2555 Madrona Ave. St Helena 94573

Chardonnay,'89, Napa Vly. $16.00 (S-Nat'l O.S.)
Merlot,'89, Napa Vly. $20.00 (3)
Red Meritage,'90, Napa Vly., Claret, Meritage (2)

NICHELINI

2950 Sage Canyon Rd. St Helena 94574

Cabernet Sauvignon,'88, Napa Vly., Nichelini Vnyd. (B-L.A.)
Johannisberg Riesling,'90, California (G-Orange)
Sauvignon Blanc,'90, California (G-Orange)
Zinfandel,'89, Napa Vly., Nichelini Vnyd. (B-Orange)

O

OAKFORD VINEYARDS

Address not available

Cabernet Sauvignon,'88, Napa Vly. (B-Orange)

OBESTER WINERY

12341 San Mateo Rd. Half Moon Bay 94019

Chardonnay,'89, Mendocino Co. (B-W. Coast)
Johannisberg Riesling,'90, Monterey Co., Ventana Vnyd. $8.00 (2)

OJAI VINEYARDS

P. O. Box 952 Oakview 93022

White Meritage,'90, Calif., Cuvee Specile, St Helene (B-Orange)

OLIVET LANE ESTATE

Address not available

Chardonnay,'90, Russian River Vly. $11.00 (S-Orange)
Chardonnay,'91, Sonoma, Cotes De Sonoma $10.00 (B-San Fran)

OLSON

3620 Road B Redwood Valley 95470

Johannisberg Riesling,'89, Mendocino Co., SLH (G-Orange)

OPUS ONE

7801 St. Helena Hwy. Oakville 94562

Red Meritage,'88, Napa Vly. $65.00 (S-Orange)

ORGANIC WINE WORKS

379 Felton Empire Road Felton 95018

Zinfandel,'91, California, LH $8.50 (4)

PAHLMEYER

P. O. Box 2410 Napa 94558

Red Meritage,'88, Napa Vly., Caldwell Vnyd., Estate (G-Orange)

PARDUCCI WINE CELLARS

501 Parducci Rd. Ukiah 95482

Cabernet Sauvignon,'88, (G-L.A.)
Chenin Blanc,'91, Mendocino Co. $6.00 (4)
Gewurztraminer,'91, Mendocino $6.00 (2)
Johannisberg Riesling,'90, North Coast $6.00 (S-Orange)
Johannisberg Riesling,'91, Central Coast $6.00 (2)
Merlot,'90, North Coast $8.00 (2)
Petite Sirah,'89, Mendocino Co. $6.00 (S-Orange)
Pinot Noir,'87, Mendocino, Cellarmaster Sel. $15.00 (B-Farmers)
Pinot Noir,'90, Mendocino Co. $6.00 (2)
Red Meritage,'86, Mendocino Co., Cellarmaster (B-Nat'l O.S.)
Sauvignon Blanc,'90, North Coast $6.00 (3)
Sauvignon Blanc,'91, Mendocino Co. (B-State Fair)
Zinfandel,'88, (B-L.A.)
Zinfandel,'90, North Coast (B-Orange)

PEACHY CANYON WINERY

Rt. 1, Box 115C Paso Robles 93446

Zinfandel,'89, Paso Robles $10.00 (4)

J. PEDRONCELLI WINERY

1220 Canyon Rd. Geyserville 95441

Cabernet Sauvignon,'88, Reserve $14.00 (S-L.A.)
Cabernet Sauvignon,'89, Dry Creek Vly. $9.50 (B-Farmers)
Chardonnay,'90, Dry Creek Vly. $9.50 (2)
Sauvignon Blanc,'91, Dry Creek Vly. Fume $7.50 (B-Farmers)
White Zinfandel,'91, Sonoma Co. $5.50 (4)
White Zinfandel,'91, Sonoma Co., Rose $5.50 (3)

PEJU PROVINCE

8466 St. Helena Hwy. Rutherford 94573

Cabernet Sauvignon,'89, Napa Vly. $14.50 (4)
Cabernet Sauvignon,'89, Napa Vly., HB Vnyd. $30.00 (4)
White Meritage,'91, Napa Vly., LH (B-State Fair)

PELLEGRINI FAMILY VINEYARDS

272 So. Maple Ave. So San Francisco 94080

Cabernet Sauvignon,'89, Cloverdale Ranch, Cuvee (3)
Chardonnay,'90, Russian River, Olivet Lane $10.00 (B-San Diego)
Chardonnay,'91, Russian River, Olivet Lane $10.00 (B-State Fair)
Sauvignon Blanc,'90, Dry Creek, Cotes De Sonoma (B-Dallas)

ROBERT PEPI WINERY

7585 St. Helena Hwy. Oakville 94562

Cabernet Sauvignon,'88, Napa Vly., Vine Hill Ranch $18.00 (3)
Chardonnay,'90, Napa Vly. $16.00 (B-San Fran)
Sauvignon Blanc,'91, Napa Vly. $10.00 (2)

PEPPERWOOD GROVE

P. O. Box 1607 Sonoma 95476

Cabernet Sauvignon,'86, California, Reserve (B-Dallas)
Cabernet Sauvignon,'90, California $5.00 (B-San Fran)
White Zinfandel,'90, California (B-Nat'l O.S.)

White Zinfandel,'91, California (B-State Fair)

MARIO PERELLI-MINETTI

1443 Silverado Trail St Helena 94574

Cabernet Sauvignon,'88, Napa Vly. (B-Orange)

PERRY CREEK VINEYARDS

Address not available

Cabernet Sauvignon,'89, Sierra Foothills (S-Orange)
Chenin Blanc,'90, El Dorado $6.00 (B-San Fran)

PESENTI WINERY

2900 Vineyard Dr. Templeton 93465

Gewurztraminer,'NV, San Luis Obispo Co. $7.00 (3)

JOSEPH PHELPS VINEYARDS

200 Taplin Road St Helena 94574

Cabernet Sauvignon,'89, Napa Vly. $18.00 (S-San Fran)
Chardonnay,'90, Napa Vly. (B-Orange)
Red Meritage,'85, Napa Vly., Insignia (B-Orange)

R. H. PHILLIPS VINEYARD

Route 1, Box 855 Esparto 95627

Cabernet Sauvignon,'90, California $8.00 (4)
Chardonnay,'91, California, Barrel Cuvee $8.00 (4)
Chenin Blanc,'91, California, Dry $5.00 (7)
Sauvignon Blanc,'91, California, Night Harvest $6.00 (2)
Sauvignon Blanc,'91, Dunnigan Hills, Night Harvest $5.00 (2)
White Zinfandel,'91, California, Night Harvest $5.00 (3)

PICONI WINERY

33410 Rancho Calif. Rd. Temecula 92591

Chenin Blanc,'91, Temecula, Country Cuvee $5.00 (B-Farmers)

PINE RIDGE WINERY

5901 Silverado Trail Napa 94558

Cabernet Sauvignon,'87, Napa Vly., Stag's Leap (B-Dallas)
Chardonnay,'90, Napa, Knollside Cuvee $16.00 (B-San Diego)
Chardonnay,'90, Stag's Leap Dist., Estate (B-San Diego)
Chenin Blanc,'89, Napa Vly., LH $14.00 (S-San Fran)
Chenin Blanc,'91, Napa Vly., Yountville Cuvee $8.00 (3)
Merlot,'89, Napa Vly., Selected Cuvee (B-San Diego)

PINNACLES ESTATE

P. O. Box 407 Rutherford 94573

Chardonnay,'90, Monterey (S-State Fair)

PIPER SONOMA

11447 Old Redwood Hwy. Healdsburg 95448

Sparkling Wine,'88, Sonoma Co., Blanc De Noirs (G-Orange)
Sparkling Wine,'88, Sonoma Co., Brut (G-Orange)

PLUME RIDGE

Address not available

Chardonnay,'90, Napa Vly. (B-Orange)

PRESTON VINEYARDS

9282 W. Dry Creek Rd. Healdsburg 95448

Cabernet Sauvignon,'88, Dry Creek Vly. $14.00 (2)
Chenin Blanc,'90, Dry Creek Vly., Estate, Dry $8.00 (S-Orange)
Sauvignon Blanc,'91, Dry Creek, Cuvee De Fume $10.00

Q

QUAFF

3364 River Road Windsor 94592

Gewurztraminer,'91, Sonoma Co. $7.00 (3)

QUAIL RIDGE CELLARS

1055 Atlas Peak Road Napa 94558

Cabernet Sauvignon,'88, Napa Vly. $16.00 (G-L.A.)
Chardonnay,'89, Napa Vly. $16.00 (B-San Diego)
Sauvignon Blanc,'90, Napa Vly. $8.00 (5)

QUINTA DO COTTA

Address not available

Chenin Blanc,'90, Lodi, Vinho Bianco (2)

QUINTESSENCE

Address not available

Cabernet Sauvignon,'89, Napa Vly. (S-Orange)
Sparkling Wine,'88, Napa Vly., Blanc De Blanc, Brut (2)

QUIVIRA VINEYARDS

4900 W. Dry Creek Rd. Healdsburg 95448

Cabernet Sauvignon,'88, Dry Creek Vly. $14.75 (4)
Sauvignon Blanc,'90, Dry Creek Vly. $10.00 (4)
Zinfandel,'89, Dry Creek Vly. (B-Nat'l O.S.)
Zinfandel,'90, Dry Creek Vly. $12.75 (4)

R

RABBIT RIDGE VINEYARDS

3291 Westside Rd. Healdsburg 95448

Chardonnay,'90, Russian River, Rabbit Ridge Ranch $12.00 (3)
Merlot,'89, Napa Vly. (B-State Fair)
White Meritage,'90, Sonoma Co., Mystique $7.00 (3)
White Meritage,'91, Sonoma Co., Mystique $7.00 (2)
Zinfandel,'90, Dry Creek Vly. $10.00 (3)

A. RAFANELLI WINERY

4685 West Dry Creek Rd. Healdsburg 95448

Cabernet Sauvignon,'89, Dry Creek Vly. $15.00 (4)
Zinfandel,'90, Dry Creek Vly. $12.00 (4)

RAMSAY

2125 Cuttings Wharf Rd. Napa 94559

Merlot,'90, Napa Vly. (B-Orange)
Petite Sirah,'89, Napa Vly. (S-L.A.)
Petite Sirah,'90, Napa Vly. (G-Orange)
Pinot Noir,'90, Napa Vly. (S-Orange)
Zinfandel,'90, Sonoma Co. (S-Orange)

RANCHO SISQUOC

Rt. 1, Box 147 Santa Maria 93454

Cabernet Sauvignon,'88, Santa Maria Vly. (2)
Chardonnay,'90, Santa Maria Vly. (S-Orange)
Johannisberg Riesling,'91, Santa Maria Vly., Estate (2)
Merlot,'89, Santa Maria Vly. (2)

KENT RASMUSSEN WINERY

2125 Cuttings Wharf Rd. Napa 94559

Chardonnay,'90, Napa Vly. $17.00 (3)

Pinot Noir,'90, Carneros $18.00 (3)

RAVENSWOOD

21415 Broadway Sonoma 95476

Cabernet Sauvignon,'89, Sonoma Co. (B-State Fair)
Cabernet Sauvignon,'89, Sonoma Co., Gregory (S-State Fair)
Merlot,'89, Sonoma Co. $15.00 (3)
Merlot,'90, Sonoma Co., Vintners Blend (B-Nat'l O.S.)
Red Meritage,'89, Sonoma Mtn., Pickberry Vnyd. $26.00 (2)
Zinfandel,'89, Sonoma Co. $11.00 (2)

RAYMOND VINEYARD

849 Zinfandel Lane St Helena 94574

Cabernet Sauvignon,'87, Napa Vly., Reserve $26.00 (3)
Cabernet Sauvignon,'88, Napa Vly. $15.00 (2)
Chardonnay,'90, California Selection $9.00 (B-Orange)
Chardonnay,'90, Napa Vly. $11.00 (4)
Chardonnay,'90, Napa Vly., Reserve $18.00 (2)
Sauvignon Blanc,'90, Napa Vly. $9.75 (4)
White Meritage,'89, Napa Vly., LH (B-State Fair)

RENAISSANCE VINEYARD

P. O. Box 1000 Renaissance 95962

Cabernet Sauvignon,'85, North Yuba, Reserve (B-Nat'l O.S.)
Cabernet Sauvignon,'86, North Yuba, Est. $15.00 (G-Nat'l O.S.)
Cabernet Sauvignon,'87, North Yuba $15.00 (2)
Johannisberg Riesling,'84, North Yuba, LH (B-W. Coast)
Johannisberg Riesling,'85, North Yuba, Estate SSLH $25.00 (2)
Johannisberg Riesling,'89, North Yuba, Est. $8.00 (B-State Fair)
Sauvignon Blanc,'84, North Yuba, Estate, LH $14.00 (3)
Sauvignon Blanc,'89, North Yuba, Estate $10.00 (S-San Diego)

RETZLAFF VINEYARDS

1356 So. Livermore Ave. Livermore 94550

Merlot,'90, Livermore Vly., Estate (2)
Red Meritage,'90, Livermore Vly., Estate (G-Orange)

REVERE VINEYARD

2456 Third Avenue Napa 94558

Chardonnay,'88, Napa Vly. $14.00 (2)

JACQUES REYNARD

Address not available

Sparkling Wine,'NV, California, Extra Dry (B-Orange)

RICHARDSON VINEYARDS

2711 Knob Hill Rd. Sonoma 95476

Cabernet Sauvignon,'89, Sonoma Vly., Horne $14.00 (4)
Cabernet Sauvignon,'90, Sonoma, Horne $14.00 (B-State Fair)
Merlot,'90, Sonoma Vly.,Carneros, Gregory $15.00 (3)
Merlot,'90, Sonoma, Carneros, Sangiacomo $15.00 (G-San Fran)
Red Meritage,'89, Sonoma/Napa Vly., Synergy $15.00 (5)
Zinfandel,'90, Sonoma Vly. $11.00 (3)

RIDGE VINEYARDS

17100 Monte Bello Rd. Cupertino 95015

Chardonnay,'90, Napa Vly., Howell Mtn. (G-Orange)

RIVER RUN

65 Rogge Lane Watsonville 95076

Cabernet Sauvignon,'89, Mendocino, Mountanos $10.00 (2)

Johannisberg Riesling,'91, Ventana Vnyd. $7.00 (B-San Fran)
Zinfandel,'89, California $9.00 (S-Nat'l O.S.)
Zinfandel,'90, California $9.00 (G-San Fran)

ROCHIOLI VINEYARD

6192 Westside Road Healdsburg 95448

Chardonnay,'90, Russian River Vly., Estate $14.00 (6)
Gewurztraminer,'91, Russian River Vly. (S-San Diego)
Pinot Noir,'90, Russian River Vly., Estate $16.00 (4)
Pinot Noir,'90, Sonoma Co. $16.00 (2)
Sauvignon Blanc,'91, Russian River Vly., Estate $9.00 (4)

ROEDERER ESTATE

4501 Highway 128 Philo 95466

Sparkling Wine,'NV, Anderson Vly., Brut (G-Orange)

ROMBAUER VINEYARDS

3522 Silverado Trail St Helena 94574

Cabernet Sauvignon,'87, Napa Vly. $15.00 (4)
Merlot,'89, Napa Vly. (S-L.A.)

ROSENBLUM CELLARS

2900 Main Street Alameda 94501

Cabernet Sauvignon,'89, Napa Vly. (B-W. Coast)
Chardonnay,'91, Napa Vly., Carneros (B-State Fair)
Petite Sirah,'89, Napa Vly. $12.00 (2)
Pinot Noir,'90, Napa Vly., George Hendry Vnyd. $13.00 (2)
Sauvignon Blanc,'91, Russian River, Hopkins Vnyd. (S-Orange)
Sparkling Wine,'90, Sonoma, Gewurztraminer (B-San Diego)
White Zinfandel,'91, Russian River Vly. (B-W. Coast)
Zinfandel,'89, Napa Vly., George Hendry Vnyd. (B-Nat'l O.S.)
Zinfandel,'90, Contra Costa Co. $10.00 (3)
Zinfandel,'90, Paso Robles $10.00 (G-San Fran)
Zinfandel,'90, Samsel Vnyd., Maggie's Reserve (S-Orange)
Zinfandel,'90, Sonoma Co. $12.00 (4)
Zinfandel,'NV, California, Vintner's Cuvee V $7.50 (2)

ROSS VALLEY WINERY

Address not available

Zinfandel,'90, Sonoma Co., Parsons' Vnyd. (B-State Fair)

ROUDON-SMITH VINEHARDS

2364 Bean Creek Rd. Santa Cruz 95066

Petite Sirah,'90, San Luis Obispo $9.00 (B-San Fran)

ROUMIGUIERE VINEYARDS

320 Johnstone Dr. San Rafael 94903

Sauvignon Blanc,'90, Lake Co. Fume $7.50 (2)

ROUND HILL CELLARS

1680 Silverado Trail St Helena 94574

Cabernet Sauvignon,'87, Napa Vly., Reserve (B-Nat'l O.S.)
Chardonnay,'90, California $7.00 (G-Orange)
Chardonnay,'90, Napa Vly., Reserve $11.00 (2)
Merlot,'89, Napa Vly., Reserve $11.00 (2)
Sauvignon Blanc,'91, Napa Vly., Fume (B-Orange)
White Zinfandel,'91, California $5.00 (B-W. Coast)
Zinfandel,'89, Napa Vly. $6.00 (4)

ROYCE VINEYARDS

1138 Apple Creek Ln. Santa Rosa 95401

Chardonnay,'90, California (2)
Merlot,'90, Napa Vly. (B-Nat'l O.S.)
White Zinfandel,'90, California (B-Nat'l O.S.)

RSV

Address not available

Red Meritage,'88, Carneros, Claret (S-Orange)
Red Meritage,'89, Los Carneros, Prop. Red $28.00 (S-San Fran)

RUSTRIDGE WINERY

2910 Lower Chiles Road St Helena 94574

Johannisberg Riesling,'90, Napa Vly., LH $12.00 (B-San Fran)

RUTHERFORD ESTATE CELLARS

Address not available

Chardonnay,'89, Napa Vly. (B-Orange)
Sauvignon Blanc,'89, Napa Vly. (B-Orange)
White Zinfandel,'90, Napa Vly. (G-Orange)

RUTHERFORD HILL WINERY

200 Rutherford Hill Rd. Rutherford 94573

Cabernet Sauvignon,'87, Napa Vly. (B-Dallas)
Cabernet Sauvignon,'87, Napa Vly., XVS (S-San Diego)
Chardonnay,'88, Napa Vly., XVS $18.00 (S-San Diego)
Merlot,'89, Napa Vly. (G-Dallas)
Sauvignon Blanc,'90, Napa Vly. $9.00 (2)

RUTHERFORD RANCH

1680 Silverado Trail St Helena 94574

Cabernet Sauvignon,'87, Napa Vly. $15.00 (2)
Chardonnay,'90, Napa Vly. $10.00 (B-Farmers)
Merlot,'88, Napa Vly. (B-Orange)

RUTHERFORD VINTNERS

1673 St. Helena Hwy. So. Rutherford 94573

Sauvignon Blanc,'88, Napa Vly. (B-Orange)

S

SAINTSBURY WINERY

1500 Los Carneros Ave. Napa 94558

Chardonnay,'90, Carneros $14.00 (B-Orange)
Chardonnay,'90, Carneros, Reserve (G-Orange)
Pinot Noir,'90, Carneros $17.00 (S-Orange)
Pinot Noir,'90, Carneros, Garnet (B-Orange)

SALAMANDRE WINE CELLARS

108 Don Carlos Drive Aptos 95003

Sauvignon Blanc,'90, Arroyo Seco $10.00 (S-San Fran)

SANFORD WINERY

7250 Santa Rosa Rd. Buellton 93427

Chardonnay,'90, Santa Barbara Co., Barrel Sel. $28.00 (2)
Pinot Noir,'89, Santa Barbara Co. $16.00 (3)
Pinot Noir,'90, Santa Barbara Co. $16.00 (2)
Sauvignon Blanc,'90, Santa Barbara Co. (S-W. Coast)

SANTA BARBARA WINERY

202 Anacapa St. Santa Barbara 93101

Cabernet Sauvignon,'89, Santa Ynez Vly., Res. (S-Orange)
Chardonnay,'90, Santa Barbara Co. $12.00 (4)
Chardonnay,'90, Santa Barbara, Reserve $20.00 (4)
Chenin Blanc,'90, Santa Ynez Vly. $8.00 (B-San Fran)
Johannisberg Riesling,'90, Santa Ynez Vly. $7.50 (2)
Pinot Noir,'90, Santa Barbara, Res. $20.00 (G-San Fran)
Sauvignon Blanc,'89, Santa Ynez Vly. $8.00 (S-San Fran)
Sauvignon Blanc,'90, Santa Ynez, LaFond, LH (G-Orange)
Zinfandel,'89, San Luis Obispo (B-W. Coast)
Zinfandel,'91, Central Coast, Beaujour $8.00 (3)

SANTA CRUZ MOUNTAIN

2300 Jarvis Road Santa Cruz 95065

Pinot Noir,'88, Santa Cruz Mtns., Estate (2)

SANTA YNEZ WINERY

P. O. Box 558 Santa Ynez 93460

Chardonnay,'90, Santa Barbara, Blake's Cuvee (S-Orange)
Johannisberg Riesling,'90, Santa Barbara, LH (B Orange)
White Zinfandel,'91, Central Coast (S-Orange)

SANTINO WINES

Rt. 2, Box 21-A Plymouth 95669

Sauvignon Blanc,'91, Amador Co. (G-Orange)
White Zinfandel,'89, Amador Co., White Harvest LH (B-Orange)
White Zinfandel,'91, Amador Co., White Harvest $6.00 (2)
Zinfandel,'88, Amador Co. (B-Dallas)
Zinfandel,'89, Amador Co., Clockspring (B-State Fair)
Zinfandel,'89, Amador Co., Grand Pere Vnyd. (2)
Zinfandel,'89, Shenandoah Vly., Grandpere $12.00 (2)

SARAFORNIA CELLARS

Address not available

Zinfandel,'88, Napa Vly. (S-Orange)

V. SATTUI WINERY

1111 White Lane St Helena 94574

Cabernet Sauvignon,'87, Napa Vly. $14.00 (2)
Cabernet Sauvignon,'87, Napa Vly., Preston $35.00 (S-Nat'l O.S.)
Cabernet Sauvignon,'88, Napa Vly., Preston $35.00 (S-San Fran)
Chardonnay,'90, Napa Vly., Carsi Vinyd., Estate $15.00 (3)
Johannisberg Riesling,'91, Napa Vly. $9.00 (5)
Johannisberg Riesling,'91, Napa Vly., Off Dry $9.25 (3)
White Zinfandel,'91, California $7.50 (5)
Zinfandel,'87, Napa Vly., Howell Mtn. Reserve $13.00 (2)
Zinfandel,'88, Napa Vly., Howell Mtn. $13.00 (2)
Zinfandel,'89, Napa Vly., Suzanne's Vnyd., Estate $12.75 (5)

SAUCELITO CANYON

1600 Saucelito Creek Rd. Arroyo Grande 93420

Zinfandel,'90, Arroyo Grande Vly., Estate $12.00 (3)

SAUSAL VINEYARDS

7370 Highway 128 Healdsburg 95448

Cabernet Sauvignon,'87, Alexander Vly. $14.00 (B-Nat'l O.S.)

SCHARFFENBERGER

307 Talmadge Rd. Ukiah 95482

Sparkling Wine,'88, Mendocino, Blanc De Blanc $22.00 (5)
Sparkling Wine,'NV, Mendocino Co., Brut $18.00 (2)
Sparkling Wine,'NV, Mendocino Co., Brut Rose (2)

SCHRAMSBERG

Schramsberg Rd. Calistoga 94515

Sparkling Wine,'85, Napa Vly., Blanc De Noirs (S-Orange)
Sparkling Wine,'87, Napa Vly., Blanc De Blancs (S-Orange)
Sparkling Wine,'87, Napa Vly., Cremant (B-Orange)
Sparkling Wine,'88, Napa Vly, Cuvee De Pinot (G-Orange)

SCHUG CELLARS

6204 St. Helena Hwy. Yountville 94599

Chardonnay,'89, Carneros, Barrel Ferm. $12.00 (B-Farmers)
Pinot Noir,'85, Napa Vly., Heinemann Vnyd., Res. (S-Nat'l O.S.)
Pinot Noir,'88, Carneros, Beckstoffer Vnyd. $13.00 (2)
Pinot Noir,'89, Carneros, Beckstoffer Vnyd. $12.00 (B-San Fran)

SEBASTIANI VINEYARDS

389 Fourth St. E. Sonoma 95476

Cabernet Sauvignon,'87, Reserve (B-L.A.)
Cabernet Sauvignon,'87, Sonoma Co. (B-W. Coast)
Cabernet Sauvignon,'88, Sonoma Co. (2)
Chardonnay,'90, Sonoma Co., Family Sel., Reserve (2)
Chardonnay,'90, Sonoma Co., Family Selection (3)
Merlot,'89, Sonoma Co., Family Selection (2)
Red Meritage,'87, Sonoma Co. (B-W. Coast)
Sparkling Wine,'87, Sonoma Co., Richard Cuneo Cuvee (2)
Zinfandel,'88, Sonoma Co. (S-State Fair)

AUGUST SEBASTIANI

389 Fourth St. E. Sonoma 95476

Cabernet Sauvignon,'NV, California $5.00 (S-Orange)
Merlot,'NV, California, Country $5.00 (3)
White Zinfandel,'NV, California, Country $5.00 (B-Orange)

SEGHESIO WINERY

14730 Grove St. Healdsburg 95448

Cabernet Sauvignon,'89, Sonoma Co. $10.00 (3)
Pinot Noir,'89, Sonoma Co. $9.00 (3)
Sauvignon Blanc,'91, Dry Creek Vly. $8.00 (G-San Fran)
White Zinfandel,'91, Northern Sonoma (G-W. Coast)
Zinfandel,'89, Sonoma Co. $7.50 (3)
Zinfandel,'90, Sonoma Co. $8.00 (2)

SELLARDS WINERY

6400 Sequoia Circle Sebastopol 95472

Chardonnay,'88, Russian River Vly. (B-W. Coast)

SEQUOIA GROVE VINEYARDS

8338 St. Helena Hwy. Napa 94558

Cabernet Sauvignon,'87, Napa Co. $16.00 (S-Orange)
Cabernet Sauvignon,'87, Napa Vly., Estate $25.00 (B-Orange)
Cabernet Sauvignon,'88, Napa Vly. $16.00 (4)
Cabernet Sauvignon,'88, Napa Vly., Estate $25.00 (4)
Chardonnay,'89, Napa Vly., Allen Fam., Estate $16.00 (2)
Chardonnay,'89, Napa Vly., Carneros $14.00 (3)

Chardonnay,'90, Napa Vly., Carneros $14.00 (2)

SHADOW CREEK

P. O. Box 2470 Yountville 94599

Sparkling Wine,'NV, California, Blanc De Noirs $11.00 (S-Orange)
Sparkling Wine,'NV, California, Brut $11.00 (B-State Fair)

SHADOW MOUNTAIN

Address not available

Chardonnay,'90, California (G-Orange)

SHAFER VINEYARDS

6154 Silverado Trail Napa 94558

Cabernet Sauvignon,'89, Napa Vly., Stag's Leap $19.00 (G-W.
Chardonnay,'90, Napa Vly. $15.00 (2)
Merlot,'89, Napa Vly. $19.00 (2)
Merlot,'90, Napa Vly. $19.00 (3)

SHENANDOAH VINEYARDS

12300 Steiner Rd. Plymouth 95669

Cabernet Sauvignon,'89, Amador Co. $9.00 (3)
Sauvignon Blanc,'91, Amador Co. $7.50 (B-Orange)
Zinfandel,'89, Amador Co. $7.50 (B-State Fair)

SIERRA VISTA WINERY

4560 Cabernet Way Placerville 95667

Zinfandel,'89, El Dorado Co., Estate (B-San Diego)

SIGNORELLO VINEYARDS

4500 Silverado Trail Napa 94558

Cabernet Sauvignon,'89, Napa Vly., Founder's Reserve $25.00 (6)
Chardonnay,'90, Napa Vly., Estate $18.00 (5)
Chardonnay,'90, Napa Vly., Founder's Reserve (B-San Diego)
Chardonnay,'90, Napa, Res., Bacchus Michelangelo (S-Orange)
Pinot Noir,'89, Napa Vly., Founder's Reserve (B-W. Coast)

SILVERADO HILL CELLARS

3105 Silverado Trail Napa 94558

Chardonnay,'90, Napa Vly., Vintage Estate (S-Orange)

SILVERADO VINEYARDS

6121 Silverado Trail Napa 94558

Cabernet Sauvignon,'89, Napa Vly., Stags Leap (B-State Fair)

SIMI WINERY

16275 Healdsburg Ave. Healdsburg 95448

Cabernet Sauvignon,'87, Alexander Vly., Reserve (S-Orange)
Cabernet Sauvignon,'88, Alexander Vly. $15.00 (B-San Diego)
Chardonnay,'89, Mendocino/Sonoma/Napa (B-Dallas)
Chardonnay,'90, Sonoma Co. (B-San Diego)
Chenin Blanc,'90, Mendocino Co. $6.50 (3)
Sauvignon Blanc,'90, Sonoma/Mendocino/Napa $8.75 (3)

ROBERT SINSKEY VINEYARDS

6320 Silverado Trail Napa 94558

Merlot,'89, Napa Vly., Los Carneros $18.00 (2)
Pinot Noir,'90, Napa Vly., Los Carneros $18.00 (2)

SCOTT SLIGER

Address not available

Chardonnay,'90, Santa Barbara Co. $15.00 (B-Orange)

SMITH & HOOK WINERY

37700 Foothill Rd. Soledad 93960

Cabernet Sauvignon,'88, Monterey, Smith & Hook (B-Nat'l O.S.)
Merlot,'88, Santa Lucia Highlands, Estate $14.00 (4)

SOBON ESTATE

14430 Shenandoah Rd. Plymouth 95669

Cabernet Sauvignon,'88, Amador Co. (2)
Sauvignon Blanc,'90, Shenandoah Vly., Fume $9.00 (S-San Fran)
Zinfandel,'89, Sierra Foothills (B-W. Coast)

SOLIS WINERY

3920 Hecker Pass Hwy. Gilroy 95002

Chardonnay,'90, Santa Clara Co., Barrel Ferm. (B-Orange)
Johannisberg Riesling,'90, Santa Clara Vly. $6.50 (B-Nat'l O.S.)

SOLITUDE

Address not available

Chardonnay,'90, Carneros, Sangiacomo Vnyd. (B-Orange)

SONOMA CREEK WINERY

23355 Millerick Road Sonoma 95476

Chardonnay,'90, Carneros, Barrel Ferm. $12.00 (4)
Chardonnay,'90, Carneros, Estate, Organic $15.00 (B-Farmers)
Chardonnay,'91, Carneros (B-State Fair)

SONOMA CUTRER

4401 Slusser Rd. Windsor 95492

Chardonnay,'90, Cutrer Vnyd. $18.00 (B-Orange)

SONOMA MISSION

Address not available

Chardonnay,'90, Sonoma Co. (S-Orange)

SONORA WINERY

P. O. Box 242 Sonora 95370

Zinfandel,'90, Sonoma Co. $9.00 (3)

ST. CLEMENT VINEYARDS

2867 St. Helena Hwy. N. St Helena 94574

Cabernet Sauvignon,'88, Napa Vly. $20.00 (2)
Cabernet Sauvignon,'89, Napa Vly. $20.00 (2)
Chardonnay,'90, Carneros Abbotts Vnyd. $18.00 (5)
Chardonnay,'90, Napa Vly. $16.00 (8)
Merlot,'89, Napa Vly. $18.00 (5)
Sauvignon Blanc,'91, Napa Vly. $10.00 (3)

ST. FRANCIS WINERY

8450 Sonoma Hwy. Kenwood 95452

Cabernet Sauvignon,'89, Sonoma Vly. $24.00 (G-State Fair)
Chardonnay,'90, Sonoma Co. $10.00 (2)
Chardonnay,'91, Sonoma Co. $10.00 (B-State Fair)
Gewurztraminer,'91, Sonoma Co. $7.50 (5)
Merlot,'89, Sonoma Vly., Estate $17.00 (2)
Zinfandel,'90, Sonoma Vly., Old Vines $12.00 (B-Farmers)

ST. SUPERY WINERY

P. O. Box 38 Rutherford 94573

Chardonnay,'90, Napa Vly., Dollarhide Ranch $13.00 (6)
Merlot,'89, Napa Vly., Dollarhide Ranch (S-San Diego)
Sauvignon Blanc,'90, Napa Vly., Dollarhide Ranch $8.50 (2)

STAG'S LEAP WINE CELLARS

5766 Silverado Trail Napa 94558

Cabernet Sauvignon,'88, Napa, Stag's Leap Vnyd. (S-State Fair)
Cabernet Sauvignon,'89, Napa Vly. (S-State Fair)
Cabernet Sauvignon,'89, Napa Vly., SLV/Fay Vnyd. $27.00 (2)
Chardonnay,'90, Napa Vly. $18.75 (3)
Chardonnay,'90, Napa Vly., Beckstoffer Ranch (B-State Fair)
Chardonnay,'90, Napa Vly., Reserve $28.00 (G-San Fran)
Sauvignon Blanc,'90, Napa, Rancho Chimiles $10.50 (B-Farmers)

STAGLIN FAMILY VINEYARDS

Address not available

Cabernet Sauvignon,'90, Napa Vly. $22.00 (B-San Fran)
Chardonnay,'89, Napa Vly. (B-Orange)
Chardonnay,'90, Napa Vly. $20.00 (2)

STANFORD

Address not available

Sparkling Wine,'NV, Calif., Governor's Cuvee, Brut (B-Orange)
Sparkling Wine,'NV, Calif., Governor's Cuvee, X-Dry (G-Orange)

STEARNS WHARF

217-B Stearns Wharf Santa Barbara 93101

Petite Sirah,'90, Central Coast (S-Orange)

STELTZNER VINEYARDS

5998 Silverado Trail Napa 94558

Merlot,'90, Napa Vly., Stag's Leap Dist. $16.50 (B-Orange)
Sauvignon Blanc,'91, Napa Vly., Oak Knoll Ranch $9.00 (B-Orange)

STERLING VINEYARDS

1111 Dunaweal Ln. Calistoga 94515

Cabernet Sauvignon,'88, Napa Vly., Diamond Mtn. (G-Nat'l O.S.)
Chardonnay,'88, Napa, Diamond Mtn. Ranch $16.00 (2)
Chardonnay,'90, Napa Vly., Estate $16.00 (B-Dallas)
Pinot Noir,'89, Carneros, Winery Lake $14.00 (2)
Pinot Noir,'90, Napa Vly., Carneros $14.00 (G-State Fair)
Red Meritage,'88, Napa Vly., Sterling Reserve $40.00 (5)
Red Meritage,'88, Napa Vly., Three Palms Vnyd. $23.00 (2)
Sauvignon Blanc,'90, Napa Vly., Estate $9.00 (B-Orange)

STEVENOT WINERY

2690 San Domingo Rd. Murphys 95247

Cabernet Sauvignon,'88, Amador Co., Grand Reserve (B-L.A.)
Cabernet Sauvignon,'89, California (B-Orange)
Chardonnay,'90, Calaveras Co., Reserve $10.00 (B-Farmers)
Merlot,'90, North Coast, Reserve $10.00 (3)
White Zinfandel,'91, Amador Co. $5.00 (2)
Zinfandel,'89, Amador Co., LH (B-Nat'l O.S.)

STONE CREEK CELLARS

539 Broadway #D Sonoma 95476

Cabernet Sauvignon,'86, Napa Vly., Special Selection (2)
Cabernet Sauvignon,'89, California $5.00 (B-Dallas)
Chardonnay,'89, North Coast (B-State Fair)
Chardonnay,'90, Alexander Vly., Estate (S-Orange)
Chardonnay,'90, Napa Vly. $9.00 (B-San Fran)
Gewurztraminer,'90, Sonoma Co., Special Sel. (4)
Merlot,'89, California, Special Selection $7.00 (S-Dallas)

Merlot,'90, California, Special Selection $7.00 (3)
Sauvignon Blanc,'91, Napa Vly. Fume, Special Sel. $6.00 (2)
White Zinfandel,'91, California $5.00 (3)

STONEGATE WINERY

1183 Dunaweal Lane Calistoga 94515

Cabernet Sauvignon,'87, Napa Vly., Est. $14.00 (G-Orange)

J. STONESTREET & SONS

337 Healdsburg Ave. Healdsburg 94558

Cabernet Sauvignon,'88, Alexander Vly. $24.00 (2)
Chardonnay,'90, Sonoma Co. $20.00 (6)
Pinot Noir,'90, Russian River Vly. $30.00 (5)

STONY RIDGE WINERY

4948 Tesla Road Livermore 94550

Cabernet Sauvignon,'89, California (2)
Cabernet Sauvignon,'89, Napa Vly., Ltd. Release $9.50 (3)
Chardonnay,'89, Napa Vly., Ltd. Release (B-Nat'l O.S.)
Chardonnay,'91, Sonoma Co. (2)
Johannisberg Riesling,'90, Arroyo Seco, Limited $5.50 (3)
Merlot,'90, North Coast, Ltd. Release $9.00 (3)
White Zinfandel,'91, California (2)

STORRS WINERY

303 Potrero St. #35 Santa Cruz 95060

Chardonnay,'90, Santa Cruz Mtns. $20.00 (3)
Gewurztraminer,'91, Monterey Co. $7.00 (S-Orange)
Johannisberg Riesling,'91, Ventana Vnyd. $7.00 (G-Orange)
Merlot,'90, Santa Clara, San Ysidro Vnyd. $13.00 (3)
Zinfandel,'90, Beauregard Ranch $12.50 (G-Orange)

STORYBOOK MT. VINEYARDS

3835 Hwy. 128 Calistoga 94515

Zinfandel,'88, Napa Vly., Estate, Reserve $19.50 (3)
Zinfandel,'89, Napa Vly. $13.00 (B-San Fran)
Zinfandel,'90, Napa Vly. $14.00 (2)

RODNEY STRONG VINEYARDS

11455 Old Redwood Hwy. Windsor 95492

Cabernet Sauvignon,'87, Alexander's Crown $17.00 (2)
Cabernet Sauvignon,'88, Alexander's Crown $17.00 (2)
Cabernet Sauvignon,'88, Sonoma Co. $11.00 (S-Dallas)
Cabernet Sauvignon,'89, Sonoma Co. $10.00 (5)
Chardonnay,'90, Sonoma Co. $9.00 (3)
Chardonnay,'90, Sonoma Co., Chalk Hill Vnyd. $13.00 (5)
Chardonnay,'91, Sonoma Co. $9.00 (B-State Fair)
Gewurztraminer,'91, Sonoma Co. $7.00 (S-Orange)
Pinot Noir,'90, Russian River Vly., River East Vnyd. $12.00 (5)
Sauvignon Blanc,'90, Sonoma, Charlottes Home Vnyd. $9.00 (3)
Zinfandel,'88, River West Vnyd., Old Vines, Estate $14.00 (4)

STUART CREEK WINERY

Address not available

Zinfandel,'89, Sonoma Vly. (B-Orange)

SUMMIT LAKE VINEYARDS

2000 Summit Lake Dr. Angwin 94508

Zinfandel,'88, Howell Mtn., Estate (2)

SUTTER HOME

277 St. Helena Hwy. So. St Helena 94574

Chardonnay,'90, California $7.00 (B-Orange)
Chenin Blanc,'91, California (B-Orange)
Zinfandel,'89, Amador Co., Reserve (B-Orange)

SWANSON VINEYARDS

1271 Manley Lane Rutherford 94573

Cabernet Sauvignon,'88, Napa Vly. $23.00 (3)
Chardonnay,'88, Napa Vly. $14.00 (G-Nat'l O.S.)
Chardonnay,'90, Napa Vly. $14.00 (B-Orange)
Merlot,'90, Napa Vly. $15.00 (3)
Pinot Noir,'88, Napa Vly. (B-State Fair)
Zinfandel,'88, Napa Vly. $12.00 (S-L.A.)

T

AFT STREET WINERY

6450 First St. Forestville 95436

Chardonnay,'90, Sonoma Co. $8.00 (5)
Merlot,'89, Sonoma Co. $11.00 (3)
Sauvignon Blanc,'90, Sonoma Co. $7.00 (B-W. Coast)

ALBOTT VINEYARD

P. O. Box 267 Carmel 93924

Chardonnay,'89, Monterey (B-Orange)

VAN TAMAS WINES

5565 Tesla Road Livermore 94550

Cabernet Sauvignon,'88, Livermore (B-W. Coast)

IFFANY HILL VINEYARDS

Address not available

Chardonnay,'90, Edna Vly. (S-W. Coast)

JSSELING VINEYARDS

2150 McNab Ranch Rd. Ukiah 95482

Cabernet Sauvignon,'90, (S-L.A.)

IVOLI

Address not available

Sparkling Wine,'NV, Napa Vly., Brut Noir (G-Orange)

OPAZ WINES

1937 Waverly Street Napa 94558

Red Meritage,'88, Napa Vly., Rouge De Trois $15.00 (4)
White Meritage,'89, Napa Vly., SSLH $8.50 (2)

OPOLOS AT RUSSIAN RIVER VINEYARDS

5700 Gravenstein Hwy., No. Forestville 95436

Petite Sirah,'88, Sonoma Co., Rossi Ranch $14.00 (B-Orange)

ARIMAR TORRES

Address not available

Chardonnay,'90, Green Vly., Don Miguel Vnyd. $25.00 (B-San Fran)

OTT'S CHAMPAGNE CELLARS

P. O. Box 1130 Modesto 95353

Sparkling Wine,'NV, California, Brut, Reserve Cuvee $7.50 (3)
Sparkling Wine,'NV, California, Extra Dry $7.50 (4)

TREFETHEN VINEYARDS

1160 Oak Knoll Ave. Napa 94558

Cabernet Sauvignon,'86, Napa Vly., Estate Res. $16.00 (S-Orange)
Cabernet Sauvignon,'87, Napa, Trefethen Vnyd. $16.00 (2)
Johannisberg Riesling,'90, Trefethen Vnyd., Estate $9.25 (2)

TRENTADUE

19170 Redwood Hwy. Geyserville 94541

Merlot,'90, Alexander Vly., Lot 1, Estate $10.00 (3)
Zinfandel,'90, Alexander Vly. $10.00 (2)

TROUT GULCH VINEYARDS

18426 Chelmsford Dr. Cupertino 95014

Chardonnay,'90, Santa Cruz Mtns. (2)

TRUCHARD VINEYARDS

Address not available

Cabernet Sauvignon,'89, Napa Vly., Carneros (S-W. Coast)
Pinot Noir,'90, Napa Vly. (S-W. Coast)

TULOCAY WINERY

1426 Coombsville Napa 94558

Cabernet Sauvignon,'87, Napa Vly., Cliff Vnyd. (2)
Cabernet Sauvignon,'88, Napa Vly., Egan Vnyd. (B-State Fair)
Chardonnay,'89, Napa Vly., De Celles Vnyd. (2)
Pinot Noir,'88, Napa Vly., Haynes Vnyd. $18.00 (B-San Diego)

TWIN HILLS RANCH WINERY

2025 Lake Nacimiento Dr. Paso Robles 93447

Cabernet Sauvignon,'88, Paso Robles, Estate (2)
White Zinfandel,'91, Paso Robles $5.25 (2)

V

M. G. VALLEJO WINERY

1883 London Ranch Rd. Glen Ellen 95442

Cabernet Sauvignon,'89, California $5.99 (2)
Chardonnay,'90, California $5.99 (2)
Chardonnay,'91, California $6.00 (S-San Fran)
Merlot,'90, California $5.99 (4)
White Zinfandel,'91, California $4.75 (6)

VALLEY OF THE MOON WINERY

777 Madrona Rd. Glen Ellen 95442

Cabernet Sauvignon,'88, Sonoma Co., Reserve $9.00 (2)
Cabernet Sauvignon,'89, Sonoma Co. $9.00 (B-State Fair)
Chardonnay,'90, Sonoma Co. $12.00 (B-Farmers)
Sauvignon Blanc,'90, Sonoma Co. $5.00 (S-State Fair)
White Zinfandel,'91, Sonoma Vly. $5.00 (3)

VALLEY RIDGE

539 Broadway #D Sonoma 95476

Sauvignon Blanc,'90, Sonoma Co. $5.00 (B-Nat'l O.S.)
Zinfandel,'88, Sonoma Co. $7.00 (3)

VAN DER KAMP CHAMPAGNE

307 Warm Springs Rd. Kenwood 95452

Sparkling Wine,'86, Sonoma Vly., English Cuvee $15.00 (7)
Sparkling Wine,'88, Sonoma Vly., Midnight Cuvee $15.00 (6)

/ENDANGE

389 4th St. E. Sonoma 95476

Chardonnay,'91, $5.00 (B-L.A.)
Sauvignon Blanc,'91, California $5.00 (2)
White Zinfandel,'91, California $5.00 (B-W. Coast)
Zinfandel,'89, California $5.00 (S-Orange)

/ENTANA VINEYARDS

2999 Monterey Salinas Hwy. Monterey 93940

Chardonnay,'89, Monterey, Gold Stripe $10.00 (S-Nat'l O.S.)
Chardonnay,'89, Monterey, Ventana, Eagle $24.00 (S-Nat'l O.S.)
Chardonnay,'90, Monterey, Crystal (B-Orange)
Chardonnay,'90, Monterey, Gold Stripe $10.00 (B-Orange)
Johannisberg Riesling,'87, Monterey, Ventana, LH (B-Nat'l O.S.)
Johannisberg Riesling,'90, Monterey, Ventana Vnyd. $7.00 (2)
Sauvignon Blanc,'89, Monterey, Ventana Vnyds. $8.00 (S-Nat'l O.S.)
Sauvignon Blanc,'90, Monterey, Estate $8.00 (4)
Sauvignon Blanc,'91, Monterey, Ventana Vnyd. $8.00 (B-San Fran)

/ICHON WINERY

1595 Oakville Grade Oakville 94562

Cabernet Sauvignon,'88, Napa Vly., Stag's Leap Dist. $24.00 (6)
Cabernet Sauvignon,'89, Napa Vly., Tenth Harvest $16.00 (4)
Chardonnay,'89, Napa Vly. $16.00 (2)
Chardonnay,'90, Napa Vly. $15.00 (7)
Merlot,'89, Napa Vly., Tenth Harvest $17.00 (3)
White Meritage,'89, Napa Vly., Chevrignon $9.60 (B-Nat'l O.S.)
White Meritage,'90, Napa Vly., Chevrignon $9.60 (4)

/ILLA HELENA

1455 Inglewood Ave St Helena 94574

White Meritage,'89, Napa Vly., Dulcinea, SSLH $15.00 (G-Orange)

ILLA MT. EDEN WINERY

620 Oakville Cross Rd. Oakville 94562

Cabernet Sauvignon,'88, California, Cellar Select $9.00 (6)
Cabernet Sauvignon,'88, Napa Vly. $9.00 (S-San Diego)
Cabernet Sauvignon,'88, Napa Vly., Reserve $12.00 (5)
Cabernet Sauvignon,'89, Napa Vly. $9.00 (S-L.A.)
Chardonnay,'90, California, Select $9.00 (4)
Chardonnay,'90, Napa Vly., Grand Reserve (B-San Diego)
Zinfandel,'89, California, Cellar Select $9.00 (G-San Fran)
Zinfandel,'90, California, Cellar Select $9.00 (7)

ILLA ZAPU

3090 Mt. Veeder Road Napa 94558

Cabernet Sauvignon,'88, Napa Vly. $19.00 (3)
Chardonnay,'90, Napa Vly. (S-Orange)

INA VISTA WINERY

14401 Chianti Road Geyserville 95441

Cabernet Sauvignon,'87, Alexander Vly. $16.00 (5)
Chardonnay,'89, Alexander Vly., Wasson Vnyd. $10.00 (5)
Merlot,'88, Alexander Vly. $11.00 (2)

WEIBEL VINEYARDS

1250 Stanford Ave. Mission San Jose 94538

Chardonnay,'90, Mendocino Co. (B-Orange)
Gewurztraminer,'90, Mendocino Co. $5.00 (S-Orange)
Sparkling Wine,'NV, Calif., Premium, Spumante (B-Orange)
Sparkling Wine,'NV, Calif., White Zinfandel $6.00 (G-Orange)

WELLINGTON VINEYARDS

P. O. Box 568 Glen Ellen 95442

Cabernet Sauvignon,'89, Sonoma, Mohrhardt Ridge (S-Orange)

WENTE BROS.

5565 Tesla Road Livermore 94550

Cabernet Sauvignon,'88, Livermore, Wente Vnyd. (B-State Fair)
Chardonnay,'90, Arroyo Seco, Riva Ranch (B-Orange)
Chardonnay,'90, Central Coast $8.00 (2)
Chenin Blanc,'90, Central Coast LeBlanc De Blancs $5.00 (5)
Johannisberg Riesling,'87, Arroyo Seco $18.00 (B-Farmers)
Johannisberg Riesling,'89, Arroyo Seco Vnyd. (2)
Johannisberg Riesling,'90, Central Coast $6.00 (B-Orange)
Sauvignon Blanc,'88, Livermore Vly., Res. $12.00 (B-San Fran)
Sauvignon Blanc,'90, Livermore Vly., Family Sel. $8.00 (B-Orange)
Sparkling Wine,'85, Arroyo Seco, Brut $10.00 (S-Nat'l O.S.)
Sparkling Wine,'NV, Arroyo Seco, Grande Brut (B-Orange)
White Zinfandel,'91, California, Wente Family Selection $6.00 (2)

WESTWOOD WINERY

1709 Carson Road Placerville 95667

Pinot Noir,'89, Napa Vly., Haynes Vnyd., Reserve (2)
Pinot Noir,'90, California (4)

WHALER VINEYARD

6200 Eastside Road Ukiah 95482

Zinfandel,'89, Mendocino, Estate $10.00 (G-San Fran)
Zinfandel,'90, Mendocino (B-W. Coast)

WILLIAM WHEELER WINERY

130 Plaza Street Healdsburg 95448

Cabernet Sauvignon,'88, Dry Creek Vly. $15.00 (5)
Chardonnay,'90, Sonoma Co. $13.00 (3)

WHITE OAK VINEYARDS

208 Haydon St. Healdsburg 95448

Chardonnay,'89, Sonoma Co., Myers Res. $20.00 (G-Dallas)
Chardonnay,'90, Sonoma Co., Myers Reserve $20.00 (4)
Chardonnay,'91, Sonoma Co. $12.95 (2)
Chenin Blanc,'90, Alexander Vly. $6.95 (2)
Sauvignon Blanc,'90, Sonoma Co. $8.95 (2)
Zinfandel,'89, Sonoma Vly. $12.95 (3)

WHITEHALL LANE WINERY

1563 St. Helena Hwy. St Helena 94574

Cabernet Sauvignon,'88, Napa Vly. $15.00 (3)
Merlot,'89, Knight's Vly., Summer's Ranch $15.00 (S-Nat'l O.S.)

WHITFORD CELLARS

4047 E. Third Avenue Napa 94558

Chardonnay,'89, Napa Vly., Haynes Vnyd., Estate (B-Orange)

WILD HORSE WINERY

P. O. Box 638 Templeton 93465

Cabernet Sauvignon,'89, Paso Robles $13.00 (2)
Chardonnay,'90, Central Coast $12.00 (S-Nat'l O.S.)
Chardonnay,'91, Central Coast $12.00 (B-San Fran)
Merlot,'90, Central Coast $14.00 (4)
Pinot Noir,'90, Santa Barbara Co. $12.00 (2)

WILDHURST VINEYARDS

11171 Highway 29 Lower Lake 95457

Chardonnay,'90, Napa Vly. (2)
Johannisberg Riesling,'91, Clear Lake (2)
Zinfandel,'90, Clear Lake (2)

. WILE & SONS

401 So. St. Helena Hwy. St Helena 94574

Cabernet Sauvignon,'87, Napa Vly. $10.00 (2)
Chenin Blanc,'91, Napa Vly. $6.00 (B-San Fran)
Merlot,'89, Napa Vly. $10.00 (2)
Sauvignon Blanc,'90, Napa Vly., Fume (B-San Diego)
Zinfandel,'90, Napa Vly. $8.00 (B-San Fran)

WINDMERE WINES

P. O. Box 1287 Healdsburg 95448

Cabernet Sauvignon,'89, Napa, Diamond Mtn. (G-W. Coast)
Chardonnay,'90, Edna Vly., MacGregor Vnyd. $13.50 (2)

WINDSOR VINEYARDS

11455 Old Redwood Hwy. Healdsburg 95448

Cabernet Sauvignon,'85, Mendocino Co., Haehl Ranch $12.00 (6)
Cabernet Sauvignon,'87, River West Vnyd. $15.00 (3)
Cabernet Sauvignon,'88, Napa Vly., Reserve $12.50 (B-Nat'l O.S.)
Cabernet Sauvignon,'88, North Coast (B-State Fair)
Cabernet Sauvignon,'88, Sonoma Co., Signature Series $18.00 (6)
Cabernet Sauvignon,'89, Sonoma Co. (3)
Chardonnay,'89, Sonoma Co., Reserve $13.00 (4)
Chardonnay,'90, Alex. Vly., Murphy Ranch $12.00 (B-Farmers)
Chardonnay,'90, Russian Rive, River Estates $11.00 (G-L.A.)
Chardonnay,'90, Russian River, Preston Ranch, Res. (B-Orange)
Chardonnay,'90, Sonoma Co., Signature Series $20.00 (6)
Chenin Blanc,'91, Sonoma Co. $6.50 (8)
Gewurztraminer,'91, Alexander Vly. $7.50 (5)
Johannisberg Riesling,'88, Russian River Vly., Estate, LH $12.00 (2)
Johannisberg Riesling,'90, Russian Riv, Le Baron $7.50 (G-Nat'l O.S.)
Johannisberg Riesling,'91, North Coast $7.00 (3)
Johannisberg Riesling,'91, Russian Riv, Le Baron $7.50 (B-W. Coast)
Merlot,'88, Russian River Vly. $12.00 (B-W. Coast)
Merlot,'89, Sonoma Co. $12.00 (4)
Petite Sirah,'87, Sonoma Co. $10.00 (4)
Pinot Noir,'87, Los Carneros $9.50 (S-Orange)
Pinot Noir,'88, Los Carneros $9.50 (B-Farmers)
Sauvignon Blanc,'88, Alexander Vly., SLH (S-Orange)
Sauvignon Blanc,'91, Alexander Vly., Fume $10.00 (3)
Sauvignon Blanc,'91, Sonoma Co., Fume (S-Orange)
Sparkling Wine,'87, Sonoma Co., Blanc De Blanc $18.00 (5)
Sparkling Wine,'87, Sonoma Co., Blanc De Noir $13.00 (3)
Sparkling Wine,'87, Sonoma Co., Brut $13.00 (4)
Sparkling Wine,'88, Sonoma Co., Brut Rose $12.00 (3)

Sparkling Wine,'88, Sonoma. Brut, Signature (S-L.A.)
Sparkling Wine,'NV, California, Extra Dry, Lot 1 $8.00 (5)
White Zinfandel,'91, Sonoma Co. $7.00 (3)
Zinfandel,'87, Russian River Vly., Blackberry Ranch $11.00 (4)
Zinfandel,'87, Sonoma Co. $7.50 (B-Orange)
Zinfandel,'88, Dry Creek Vly., Reserve $10.00 (4)

WINDWALKER

7360 Perry Creek Somerset 95684

Chenin Blanc,'91, El Dorado, Estate, Dry (S-Orange)

WINTERBROOK WINERY

4851 Buena Vista Road Ione 95640

Sauvignon Blanc,'91, Sonoma Co. $6.50 (B-Orange)
White Zinfandel,'91, North Coast $5.00 (B-State Fair)

WOODBRIDGE

4614 W. Turner Rd. Lodi 95640

Chenin Blanc,'91, California $5.00 (S-Orange)
White Zinfandel,'91, California $5.00 (B-Orange)
Zinfandel,'90, California $7.00 (S-Orange)

WOODEN VALLEY WINERY

4756 Suisun Valley Road Suisun 94585

Merlot,'NV, Suisun Vly. (B-State Fair)

WOODSIDE VINEYARDS

340 Kings Mtn. Road Woodside 94062

Cabernet Sauvignon,'NV, Keenan & Delucci Vnyds. (B-Orange)
Chardonnay,'90, Santa Cruz Mtns., Estate $14.00 (S-Farmers)

Y

YORK MOUNTAIN WINERY

Rt. 2, Box 191 Templeton 93465

Cabernet Sauvignon,'86, San Luis Obispo $14.00 (B-San Diego)
Pinot Noir,'87, San Luis Obispo, Reserve $16.00 (4)
Pinot Noir,'89, San Luis Obispo Co. (S-Orange)

Z

ZACA MESA WINERY

Foxen Canyon Rd. Los Olivos 93441

Chardonnay,'89, Santa Barbara Co., Reserve $16.50 (4)
Chardonnay,'90, Santa Barbara Co. $11.00 (3)
Chardonnay,'90, Santa Barbara Co., Reserve $16.50 (B-Orange)
Johannisberg Riesling,'90, Santa Barbara Co., LH (B-Orange)
Johannisberg Riesling,'91, Santa Barbara Co. (S-Orange)
Pinot Noir,'89, Santa Barbara Co., Reserve $16.00 (2)

ZD WINES

8383 Silverado Trail Napa 94558

Cabernet Sauvignon,'89, Napa Vly. $16.00 (4)
Chardonnay,'90, California $20.00 (3)
Pinot Noir,'90, Napa Vly., Carneros $17.00 (2)

STEPHEN ZELLERBACH VINEYARD

4611 Thomas Road Healdsburg 95448

Chardonnay,'90, Sonoma Co., William Baccala (S-San Diego)